Far from Home

poems of faith, grief and gladness

Andrew Lansdown

An Even Before Publishing Book
Wombat Books

Far from Home: Poems of Faith, Grief and Gladness

An Even Before Publishing book
Published by Wombat Books
P.O. Box 1519, Capalaba, Qld 4157, Australia
www.evenbeforepublishing.com

ISBN: 978-1-921633-14-0

Cover illustration: The Caravans – Gypsy Camp near Arles (1888, Oil on canvas) by Vincent van Gogh

Back cover photograph: Dwight A Randall

Design and layout: Rochelle Manners

National Library of Australia Cataloguing-in-Publication entry

Author:	Lansdown, Andrew Trevor, 1954-
Title:	Far from home : poems of faith, grief and gladness / Andrew Lansdown.
Edition:	1st ed.
ISBN:	9781921633140 (pbk.)
Dewey Number:	A821.4

For my mother, Lois Regina Lansdown,
and my father, Colyn Trevor Lansdown,
who gave me a home and a glimpse of the Homeland

My mother often told me, angels bonded your life away
She said I would accomplish, but trust in God and pray
I'm on the King's Highway, I'm travelling everyday
'Cause I just can't keep from crying sometimes

Blind Willie Johnson, 'Lord, I Just Can't Keep From Crying'

For we are strangers before thee, and sojourners, as were all our fathers:
Our days on the earth are as a shadow, and there is none abiding.

David, The Holy Bible, 1 Chronicles 29:15 (KJV)

Andrew Lansdown was born in 1954 in Pingelly, a wheatbelt town 120 kilometres south-east of Perth, Western Australia, where he currently lives with his family. He studied at Curtin University of Technology and Murdoch University and has worked as a TAEF tutor, a prison education officer, a pastor and an editor. He is the author of ten books of poetry and five books of fiction. His poetry has been widely published in magazines, newspapers and anthologies. He has won the Western Australian Premier's Prize for Poetry (twice) and the Adelaide Festival's John Bray National Poetry Award.

Highly respected for his imagist and nature poetry, Lansdown is also acclaimed for his poems dealing with family, faith and the human condition. The eminent Australian poet, Les Murray, has said: "Many of Andrew Lansdown's poems have the power to bless, to unsettle now with mysterious calm, now with the deep resonance of poetry. Of all Australian imagists, he is the one with the broadest and warmest human sympathy, and no one writes of family love with more tenderness than he. Nor does anyone write with more perceptive courage about the dark things that move behind idyll, or the bland merciless enemies of human happiness" (from the back cover blurb of *The Grasshopper Heart*).

Also by Andrew Lansdown

Poetry
Homecoming
Counterpoise
Windfalls
Waking and Always
The Grasshopper Heart
Between Glances
Primary Loyalties (with Hal Colebatch & Peter Kocan)
Fontanelle
Warrior Monk
Consolations
Little Matters
Birds in Mind: Australian nature poems

Children's Poetry
A Ball of Gold

Short Stories
The Bowgada Birds
The Dispossessed

Poems, Stories, Essays
Abiding Things

Novels
With My Knife (USA edition, *Beyond the Open Door*)
Dragonfox
The Red Dragon

Acknowledgements

Many poems in this collection have been published in the following magazines and newspapers: *Abundant Life; The Age; Alive Magazine; The Alternative; Amity; Antipodes* (USA); *Artlook; The Australian Baptist; The Briefing; The Eye's Habit; The Bulletin; The Canberra Times; Case; Christians Writing; The Courier-Mail; Crosslight; Family Matters; Fremantle Arts Review; The Horatian; Island; Life Insight; Life News; Linq; Lynx: A Journal of Linking Poets* (USA); *Marginata; Mate* (New Zealand); *Meanjin; Micropress Yates; New Life; Northern Perspective; On Being; Overland; Poetry Australia; Quadrant; Southern Review; Studio; Sydney Morning Herald; This Australia; Verse* (Scotland); *The Weekend Australian; The West Australian; Westerly; The Western Review; The Western Word; Writing Australia; Zadock Perspectives.*

Some poems in this collection have also been published in the following anthologies: (1) *Playing With Fire: A Natural Selection of Religious Poetry*, ed, Susan Dwyer (Dublin: Villa Books, 1980). (2) *Quarry: a selection of contemporary western australian poetry*, ed, Fay Zwicky (Fremantle Arts Centre Press, 1981). (3) *Hemisphere Annual — III*, ed, Kenneth Russell Henderson (ACT: Commonwealth Department of Education, 1982). (4) *Instructions for Honey Ants and Other Poems*, ed, Paul Kavanagh (Mattara anthology; University of Newcastle, 1983). (5) *An Anthology of Christian Verse*, ed, Francis Byrne (Adelaide: Rigby, 1983). (6) *Indo-Australian Flowers*, ed, V.S. Skanda Prasad (Mangalore: Chetana Books, 1984). (7) *Poem of Thanksgiving and other poems*, ed, Paul Kavanagh (Mattara anthology; University of Newcastle, 1985). (8) *POEMS Selected from The Australian's 20th Anniversary Competition*, ed, Judith Rodriguez and Andrew Taylor (Sydney: Angus & Robertson, 1985). (9) *Portrait: a west coast collection*, ed, B.R. Coffey and Wendy Jenkins (Fremantle Arts Centre Press, 1986). (10) *The New Oxford Book of Australian Verse*, ed, Les A. Murray (Melbourne: Oxford University Press, 1986). (11) *Anthology of Australian Religious Poetry*, ed, Les A. Murray (Blackburn: Collins Dove, 1986; reprinted 1991). (12) *Wordhord: A Critical Selection of Contemporary Western Australian Poetry*, ed, Dennis Haskell & Hilary Fraser (Fremantle Arts Centre Press, 1989). (13) *Zik Avstralskih Slovencev - 1988: Anthology of Australian Slovenes – 1988*, ed, Jose Preseren et al (Sydney: Slovenian-Australian Literary & Art Circle, 1988). (14) *Australia Antologio*, ed, Alan Towsey (Pizo, Italy: Edistudio, 1988). (15) *Christmas Crackers: Australian Christmas Poetry*, ed, Ann Weld (Norwood: Omnibus Books, 1990). (16) *The Oxford History of Australia: Volume 5, 1942-1995 – The Middle Way*, Geoffrey Bolton (Melbourne: Oxford University Press, 1990; second edition, 1996). (17) *New Life Digest 1993*, ed, Bob Thomas (Blackburn: New

Life Australia, 1992). (19) *Chapters into Verse: Poetry in English Inspired by the Bible – VOLUME TWO: Gospels to Revelation*, eds Robert Atwan and Laurance Wieder (Oxford: Oxford University Press, 1993). (20) *Whispering in God's Ear: A New Collection of Poetry for Children*, ed, Alan MacDonald (Oxford: Lion Publishing, 1994). (21) *The Lion Christian Poetry Collection*, ed, Mary Batchelor (Oxford: Lion Publishing, 1995). (22) *Sudden Alchemy*, ed, Patricia Darby (Cottesloe: Fellowship of Australian Writers, 1998). (23) *No Strings Attached*, eds, Jeff Guess and Fiona Johnston (North Paramatta: Eremos Institute, 1999). (24) *The Yellow Star of Life*, ed, Andrew Lansdown (Nollamara: Life Ministries, 2003). (25) *The Best Australian Poems 2004*, ed, Les Murray (Melbourne: Black Inc, 2004). (26) *A Treasury of Christian Poetry: 700 Inspiring & Beloved Poems*, ed. Mary Batchelor, (Gramercy, 2004) (27) *The Best Australian Poems 2005*, ed, Les Murray (Melbourne: Black Inc, 2005). (28) *Studio*, ed, Paul Grover (Albury: Studio, 2006). (29) *The Best Australian Poems 2006*, ed, Dorothy Porter (Melbourne: Black Inc, 2006). (30) *The Road South: An Anthology of Contemporary Australian Poetry*, ed, Ron Pretty (Bengal Creations Pvt Ltd, 2007). (31) *GROW: Under the Southern Cross*, eds, Anne Hamilton and Lyn Hurry (Kenmore, Qld: Writerlynks Grow, 2008). (32) *School Certificate English*, ed, Paul Grover (Oxford University Press, 2009).

Some poems in this collection have also been broadcast on the following radio stations/programs: Australian Broadcasting Corporation, *A First Hearing*; Australian Broadcasting Corporation, *The Poet's Tongue*; Australian Broadcasting Corporation, *PoeticA*.

Over half the poems in *Far From Home* are previously uncollected poems. The other poems (some in revised form) have been selected from Andrew's earlier poetry collections: *Homecoming* (Fremantle: Fremantle Arts Centre Press, 1979); *Counterpoise* (Sydney: Angus & Robertson Publishers, 1982); *Windfalls* (Fremantle: Fremantle Arts Centre Press, 1984); *Waking and Always* (Sydney: Angus & Robertson Publishers, 1987. Reprinted by Picaro Press, Warners Bay, 2007); *The Grasshopper Heart* (Sydney: Collins/Angus & Robertson Publishers, 1991); *Between Glances* (Port Melbourne: William Heinemann Australia, 1993); *Fontanelle* (Melbourne: Five Islands Press, 2004); *Warrior Monk* (Warners Bay: Picaro Press, 2005).

The poet acknowledges with gratitude that many poems in this collection were written with the financial assistance of the Literature Board of the Australia Council for the Arts.

Australian Government

Australia Council for the Arts

Contents

THE GOD OF THE GLIMPSES:
A SEQUENCE OF POEMS ON THE PROPHET ELIJAH

Distress

She shares her burden—
a small boy with autism,
just now diagnosed.
And my eyes embarrass me
as we speak, until
I must turn my head to hide
my heart. Oh but why,
when I hardly know her, why
do I feel this hurt
at her hurt? I remember
a sage's maxim:
'the feeling of distress is,'
he declared, 'the root
of benevolence.' Yes—and
also the reverse:
feelings of benevolence
are the root of our distress.

Prayer

Oh, for my mother in her pain,
Almighty and all-loving Lord,
I come to plead with you again.

For years her body's been a bane
That's put all gladness to the sword:
Oh, for my mother in her pain!

Too much misery makes a stain
To black all light and block all laud:
I come to plead with you again.

Today at least relieve the strain
And give reprieve as a reward,
Oh, for my mother in her pain.

I know there is no other Name.
Despite the fact my faith is flawed,
I come to plead with you again.

Although my many sins maintain
That I deserved to be ignored—
Oh, for my mother in her pain
I come to plead with you again!

In Transit

for Mike Kelly

Two deaf women are talking on the train,
their dumb speech dancing
from their hands—an astonishing display

of synaesthesia. On this journey
speech has jettisoned me, finger and tongue.
I am too far from home.

Through the window, briefly, a row
of pines—huge, lopsided, limbs hewn back
from the line, trunks studded with stumps.

In the seat facing mine, a young woman
is asleep. Her head droops from her neck
like a cabbage chrysanthemum on a tall stem.

Her face is hidden, but her hands
are translucent-white, and twitch
like spent moths in the cloth of her lap.

The boomgate's thin bell disturbs her
as we race through a crossing. Her neck stiffens,
lifts the lolling head. But her eyes

remain blanketed in their black beds.
Tiredness is a treason in her body
betraying her to sleep among strangers.

Perhaps she is dying. Indeed
this train is death in transit.
One by one, these people will die.

And so will I. I try not to imagine
the accumulated sorrow crammed
into this railcar. We will grieve

those we love because we live
and must die. Why? And what
does deaf or death matter

if we are mere matter? Uprooted
from the pillaged earth, the pines
stand truncated in my mind;

the young woman still droops and dreams;
the dumb women still speak.
We are strangers before You,

hollowed or hallowed by hurt. Father,
the years yield me to yearning
while I tarry in transit to You.

Far from Home, the Blower

Close off one end of the didgeridoo
and look down the other—
that's how black he is, this Kimberley man.
He has come to the school for the didgeridoo.
He wants to take it back to his cell,
but I cannot give him permission
immediately. This is a maximum security prison:
procedures must be observed. So
he is playing it now in the literacy room.
I tell the officers he will be staying
for the afternoon. He is playing it now.
His eyes are closed and he is tapping
the plastic seat with his thumbnail
as the pipe drones at his feet.
Abruptly, in a gesture of harmony,
he breaks his rhythm. *That lillgah,*
he says. I do not understand.
Lillgah, he says, slowly, several times.
I cannot get it right. *Lillgah—like tuning.*
Making didgeridoo same as singer.
He plays again. A singer silent to me
is chanting in the channels of his ear.
He listens, trying to match his music
to the key and rhythm of the voice.
We always do this, start
with lillgah. If the singer not happy
with one blower, he get another.
Me a deep blower. He blows again. Indeed
the drone is deep. But I never knew
it could be otherwise. *Some singers are high.*
You know? Clear. He throws his head back,
taps his throat, and sings—high, nasally,

rhythmic, in 'language'.
I know this singing, but its meaning
is ancient and alien. He is singing
and we are in harmony. I do not
ask for meanings. But I say,
Sing low then, Simon. And he sings
low and husky, unlike anything
I have heard before. *The blower*
must be the same. See?
He plays again. A different rhythm.
An officer comes in, jangling
his keys. O freedom! I do not look up.
The didgeridoo drones vibrantly,
striking up a resonance in my soul.
Taut or slack, spiritual chords
are strung across the hollow
at the heart of every man.
No man is mere matter—therefore
the Dreaming. 'Kudda, brother,'
one of the tribal men from Kalgoorlie way
calls me. A man from Noonkanbah Station
greets me behind these walls as 'Papaji,
brother.' Simon does not call me 'brother',
but he is playing the didgeridoo
for me. He breaks off suddenly. *Now*
the young girls come in. Jdirree-jdirree.
He flicks his hands, makes a few staccato
movements with his torso. *Wanga.*
That the Law. The women start first.
He begins again, the familiar droning
tempered by new rhythms and sounds.
And somewhere in the didgeridoo
a brolga begins to dance and cry.
The men this time. First the brolga
dance. He stops again. *Now*

a dingo. She crying for her pup. And
distant through the droning, a dingo
barks and howls in the hollow
of the didgeridoo. *When I was initiated ...*
He is rehearsing his life.
And I am a cut and ochred
hollow branch: he speaks into me
evoking a sympathy that, in turn, stirs
his heart to a symphony of longing.
When I am made a man, the blower
he's playing all day. Never stop.
He be giving me his wind.
And they give me a didgeridoo, to be
a blower. But I never play
all day for initiation. I never be picked
to play all night for corroboree.
I only play short time. For fun.
You know? Maybe for white people too.
For fun. Like frogs. Gningi-gningi.
I can't catch the words.
He is sharing unfamiliar things
in a voice too quiet and quick. *A good blower,*
he cut his tongue with spinifex.
He pokes out his tongue. It is very pink
against his purple lips. He runs his thumbnail
down the tip. Yours cut? I ask.
No. Too fat. But good blower,
he listens. He hears. He gets the wisdom of it.
He cuts his tongue, gets plenty sounds.
Plenty wind. Like tortoise. Like crocodile.
You know? His gaze is distant.
He is dreaming. *To be a blower,*
he says, to be a didgeridoo-man
is good. You know? Get respect. Get proudness.

Snake with Angel

When it dived, the dabchick, I ran towards
the swamp, wanting to get closer to see better
before the bird surfaced and saw me—
I sprinted towards the swamp, my eyes
on the black hole in the bright-light-green
weed-covered water where the dabchick had dived—
and running I was not looking at the ground
I was treading and trod within a fraction
of a snake, a tiger snake—big, black-backed
and lightly banded from the orange belly—
by my foot it flicked up,
reared up like a jack jarred from its box,
sprang up and flattened its head
in fear and fury, flattened its face
like a little-hooded cobra charmed
from its basking by the pipe of my leg—
and I staggered off balance like a top
struck while spinning—I stumbled back
expecting through the long seconds
the twin pinholes of poison, oh
expecting—but it teetered, turned, tumbled
down and trickled into the rushes
away from me—and I think, I like to think
an angel, my angel, the angel assigned to me
stepped in to stop the snake from striking me!

Mercy

Across the footpath (tidy
as Euclid's brain
bar the rude little daisy
bold between two slabs)
the hose
follows itself   and

coming suddenly upon its end
throws a tantrum
before a regiment of roses.
                              But

back along its torso,
in the middle of the path,
a pin-prick spray
sets the daisy dancing.

Timphony

Weird to be here to hear,

in this field of wild lupins
laden with seed and lost
for harvest, this low symphony
of simple percussion:

the click of castanets
as dry pods dehisce
and discharge a timpani,
a timphony of seeds

to complement
the rattle of maracas
as the unpopped pods
shake in the arrhythmic air.

Waking and Always

Naomi, six months

Where has she gone? I do not hold her
as she sleeps in my arms. The tides of air
lift and let go her chest
with a delicacy that reminds me of death.
So slender, each breath! She is hot
and the sweat glistens like ground glass
on her scalp. Her eyelids are almond petals,
white, exquisitely veined with pink.

Finer than her eyelashes are fine,
yet greater than the delta of the Nile,
are the rivulets of blood in the hoods
of her eyes. The mastery of her!
No human design can hide the design in her.
She holds me as I hold her while she is held
by sleep. Her eyelids flinch and flicker,
brushed by the bright blackness of dreams.

Darling, it seems they would have us believe
that, back beyond the generations, you
and I and they—we all—were spawned
spontaneously from an inorganic soup.
They say it is 'scientific'. But I know
it is unproven and unprovable, believable
only by faith. And it is a faith that fails
the facts. The facts, say, of your eyelids.

Child, I do not believe your eyelids
or the dreams above which they flutter
are accidental—a mere coincidence
of chemicals and light, a serendipity
of time and matter. I cannot believe.
I lack the faith. Daughter, dream this
true dream: Your spirit is the wick of Yahweh,
your body, the wax of His make and moulding.

Dream this waking and always. And burn,
little candle, burn brightly in the coming night!

Sehnsucht

Everyone else is asleep
and I am up this early
only to keep my small son from crying.

I carry him down to the river.
A slight mist lingers by the bend.
Trees stand on their heads in the still water.

Has he seen a river before?
I can't remember.
He raises his hand,

reaching for it.
He looks back at me
to make sure I have seen it.

How can anyone find anything so amazing?
Yet it's not just the river:
stones, leaves, chickens, fire—

things I still love
though they've fallen familiar—
fill him continually with joy and wonder.

Oo! Oo! he says
as if it hurts him
here in my arms, seeing the river

for the first time.
And a familiar strangeness
grips my heart

and I sing to him
Jesus loves the little children
to keep from weeping.

Absence

'And Daddy, you know what?
I'm a bit lonely about you.'

From 3,000 miles away,
her voice so sweet and clear.

For Grace

Grace is out of grace
for pestering her father.
We are discussing
Important Matters and have
no time for prattle
or play. Grace is out of grace.
Forsaking us, she
clambers onto a carved chest
in the bay-window,
rests her face against the pane,
the crocheted curtains
caped loose across her shoulders.
Outside, a woman
wavers while walking to wave
to a child alone
at a window. Grace's hands
flutter like sparrows
then fall still upon the sill
as the lady leaves.
Even sparrows, Jesus said,
do not fall unseen.
Look then, Father, in the lace
while I pester you for Grace.

Sometimes in the Dark

There is, someone claims,
a pup in the prison.
And then a *yap!* confirms
it. Who now can work?

The women, the inmates,
are excited. The welfare
officer has passed the gates
with a pup at her heels!

It is trotting along
the verandah, towards
H Block—springy, strong
and defiantly doggy.

'Oh!' says one 'girl'
who is serving time
for murder. Memories whirl.
'Oh, I haven't seen a dog

for nearly four years!'
The bars are no barrier
to the pup. It peers
through and the murderess

picks it up and hugs
it with a hard urgency.
It licks her face. No drugs
could put that distance

in her eyes. She thinks,
Four years and six to go.
She shakes her head, blinks
and says for consolation:

'But sometimes in the dark,
far off, I hear them bark.'

In Prison

At least in here,
she said, *he*

can't get at me
or make me do

something
I don't want to.

Tanka about Pain

1. Chronic Pain

Stupid, really,
to say it, given the pain
must be and is ...
Yet I feel compelled to cry
one more time: *Unbearable!*

2. Killers

Once again pain
has conquered my pain-killers.
So many down!
I send reinforcements, hardly
caring if they kill ... pain or me.

3. Giving Comfort

In lovingkindness
my friend calls to ask after
the state of my pain.
And to comfort him I say,
'It's not quite so bad today.'

Measure

I wonder often
these days how much I am loved.
I am well aware
for some the answer's, 'Not much!'
Yet is there nowhere
someone who can say how much?
At the cross, Jesus
himself stretches his free hand
to the nailing place.
He seems to gesture, 'This much!'
But a doubt undoes
my judgment of the measure ...
Perhaps he means, 'More than this!'

Golgotha

Finally, one arrives at the place
of the skull because there is nowhere
else to go. And there before the face
of bone one pauses in despair.

The culmination of all evil
is displayed before one's eyes.
Man's heart conspired with the devil
and cared little for disguise.

Yet if, at the sight of the Cross,
a light is struck on the rough of the brain
and the mind conceives all bar this is vain,

there comes a voice that reassures: Thus
is the seed of tenderness sown
in the cleft of the heart of stone.

White Gum

This white-barked wandoo,
this most-Australian gum,
rises through the air, rigid
with wood, latent with post

and cross-beam. It is fitting,
really, that this eucalypt,
this kinstree to the Cross
of the Son of God, should be

an incarnation of the light
of the sun—the same sun
the world over, the millennia
long. Run your hand up the trunk

towards the limbs you cannot
reach. There are no splinters
in the bark. Go ahead, touch
the wood, the living timber

the nails have yet to pierce.

Communion

for Iain & Liz Parker

The garden is dry but the birdbath
brims with black water from the bottom
of the dam. Beside the gravel path

two stumps beckon small birds from the bush,
invite with a voice they never had
when fused, infused with the sap's green push.

One, on its plane, bears sugar and grain.
The other, in a glazed clay dish, holds
the dark dregs of last winter's light rain.

A neat, white-naped honeyeater takes
a bath. A fantail alights to flirt.
On the flat grass nearby, like snow flakes,

a fall of rolled oats. Be still. Don't speak.
Share this communion: a blue wren is
breaking a white wafer with his beak.

Duty

That kingfisher framed
in the knot of a white gum,

buff on its belly,
azure on its wings:

forgive this poor
tired heart of mine,

my King, that it cannot
this moment praise you

as that bird declares
you desire and deserve.

Black Bamboo

i

Empathy today
with the ebony bamboo—
this empty feeling.

ii

This feeling—something
that's escaped from the centre
of a bamboo cane.

iii

Hollow ... I suppose
the bamboo by my window
always feels this way.

iv

Again I wake
with a hollow feeling—oh,
my bamboo heart!

v

Hollow, like the black
bamboo ... if only I had
its composure, too.

vi

Lord, may not music
come from emptiness? Oh, make
a flute of my heart!

Idyll
Boyup Brook, Western Australia

The fields are green with clover;
ewes gives suck to their lambs;
wood ducks graze with their ducklings;
and dabchicks dive in the dams.

Robins set fire to the roadside;
rosellas fly up from the oats;
kingfishers reel blue from the skyline;
and magpies toss tunes from their throats.

Shorn sheep line a creek like sandbags;
frogs rollick in the rushes and croak;
and among the trees in the orchard
almonds signal spring with white smoke.

I'd planned in the lines of my pastoral
to deny the encroachment of death:
the sheep are not trucked to the slaughter;
the birds are not robbed of their breath;

the frogs are safe from the heron;
the petals from the almonds don't fall.
But beauty in the end's an illusion,
an embroidery on the fringe of a pall.

So it's futile to think in the future
this poem will preserve what I saw
and readers will see the scene through me
unaware that I see it no more.

Jaded

All is not jaded,
the wildflowers say—but I
am not persuaded.
Will you say so bye and bye
when your faces are faded?

Sheep

Only three days since
they were shorn and already
their whiteness is gone.
Still, who of us has managed
even that long in this world?

Each Lily

Each arum lily
beside the dam's amphitheatre
is holding aloft
(as at carols by candlelight)
a yellow flame in a white cup.

Navigation

Though navigators
can find their way by the stars,
I look and am lost.
The only place they lead me,
my Sovereign, is home to you.

Marri with Nuts

After rain
sometimes gumnuts
—the big-bowled,

boldly-rimmed
nuts of the marri
—smoulder

as if packed
with tobacco
and set alight.

Or, which is
more beautiful,
as if each nut

were a thurible,
a wooden censer,
wafting incense.

Indeed, this
green-robed tree
is a thurifer

unconsciously
praising God
most consciously

through me.

Creators

Having created
the bamboo, God created
in His likeness
human beings, and seeing
bamboos growing
they straightaway imagined
xylophones, wind-chimes and flutes!

Parable

for Leroy Randall

Plant a seed, reap a song:
such are the ways of God.

Jesus said his kingdom
is like a mustard seed

which when buried rises
to a tree, and the birds

alight in its branches.
So, from a grain, a surge

of sap and shade, a haunt
of gladness and surprise.

Oh, beyond all desire,
the tree of God abounds

with nests—and a choir!

Apart from Blood

for my father

I do not know when I first knew
I loved you, but from my youth
I have loved you more and more.

And while, apart from blood,
there are reasons,
surely one is to the fore:

Your life has spoken
the mysterious grammar of godliness,
the deep logic of love and law.

Father, if in eternity I have a place,
it is because (no matter how jaded)
I first saw Jesus in your face.

Man of Sorrows

Not so that you would notice—
unless, like me, you were sitting beside him—
my father is weeping. He has removed
his glasses and is dabbing his eyes.
We are singing a hymn—one thousand Christians
singing to our Saviour. But my father
is weeping. What grief has gripped his heart?
His mortality? His two sons who are dead?
The disunity in the Church or the dishonour
in the nation? Perhaps it is just
the unspeakable loneliness of righteousness.
Yes, this most of all. I dare not look at him
lest I, too, should weep. Certainly, Christ
is our Comforter. And He needs to be, too,
being, as He is, the chief cause of our sorrow.

Family

'There's no one as good as us,
is there, Mum?' my grandmother said
my mother said when she was young.
So, without forethought or fuss,

she defined, as only children can,
her family and herself: familiar
with the lineaments of love, she felt
at home in her home. As a man

I hear her speak, this woman who
was once a girl my father never
knew. My mother, in all her grief
and grace. As if they were new

she remembers the old sureties
and shares them now with me—
this woman whom I love because
like Christ she first loved me.

Mother, oh, be assured of this:
what is true for you is true for me
(and may my children say the same),
'There's no one, not one as good as us!'

On Poetry

for William Hart-Smith

As we sit talking
about poetry

my son (still months
from walking)

lounges without a care
on my knee, fronts

my old friend with
a vacant stare,

spasmodically stops
our talking with

a short sigh,
and lifts and drops

his foot rhythmically
on the flat of my thigh.

Courage

i

Shouting and shooting—
my boisterous boys playing at
goodies-and-baddies.

ii

Yes, my little boys,
against the impending day,
play at being brave.

Admiration

i

Scuffling with my sons.
'You're the strongest in the world!'
Dear, deluded things.

ii

My littlest sons—
for years yet they will keep on
looking up to me.

Behind the Veil

How often my grandparents allude to death, now.
The simplest plans and preparations for the new year
they preface and conclude: If we're still here.
Age, bodily decrepitude will not allow
illusion. Before death, all things somehow
become transient and grave. Joy and regret
marry each other at the altar of memory. Who can forget
our mortality? Even youths and social visionaries will bow.

For all this, my grandparents are at peace, hoping for the face
of Christ our Saviour. Death will degrade:
even for the redeemed, this peppercorn must be paid.
But He is the resurrection: they are sure of His power and grace.
Still, they are lonely in the shadow of death.
Oh for His face, hidden by the veil of each breath!

He Knows a Place

He knows a place we cannot share,
a wholly black and boundless space,
and when he went he drew us there.

It is the rift left in a tear,
a bullet or a blade's wet trace,
this place he knows we cannot share.

It is the darkness called despair
that none survive except by grace.
And when he went he drew us there.

Don't go, beloved! Oh, beware!
Don't turn your heart and set your face
upon that place we cannot share!

Sorrow and sickness were the fare
that gave him passage to that place.
And when he went he drew us there.

It barely counts how much we care.
This is the fact we must embrace:
he knows a place we cannot share,
and when he went he drew us there.

In Memoriam

i

We knew something was wrong
because of the blood
but we had not expected this.
'I can't find a heart beat,'
the doctor says. 'I'm sorry.'

ii

Dear child you died
in the secret safe place
alone. What did you suffer?
How could we have known?
Oh son, daughter, I'm sorry.

iii

I collected the images
from the ultrasound, the record,
child, of your short life
and long death. I burnt them
to spare your mother. I'm sorry.

Hurt

A woman singing
Mississippi John Hurt blues ...
She croons his ballad
about angels, death and dirt,
laying me away with hurt.

Fathers

Over the air waves,
weeping, a father whose son
killed by negligence
another father's daughter ...
Oh, Father—justice, mercy!

Into Darkness

I am walking at dusk in the lull
between rain. Slugs blot
the footpath. Faintly luminous,
flowers reflect the residual light.

I pass pink, loose-petalled roses,
clumped on bushes like soggy tissues,
and white cabbage chrysanthemums,
battered to the ground and spattered

with sand. I am breaching the border
of twilight, trying not to fear
the fate of my children as they face
the frontier. Like the planet,

my thoughts spin nightward. Retreating,
the day destroys the third dimension,
deprives the world of depth.
Trees turn black. In silhouette

a spindly eucalypt sculptures the rain,
its slender leaves flouncing
in squalls in the hesitant wind.
Through radiating tiers of branches

a Norfolk Island pine points the way
to heaven, holds highmost a cross.
I am walking into darkness. Colours
are draining away, shapes dissolving.

All the old certainties are lost.
Above, the moon is a spillage of light
mopped up by the clouds. The moon
with its meaning: the sun that shone

is still shining. I am walking
through the dark on the turning world.

Listening to Louis

Though he is dead, Louis Armstrong
rasps out, 'What a wonderful world!'

then shifts into a slow rendition of
'Nobody knows the trouble I've seen.'

Just how true these words are, and
sad as true, 'Nobody knows but Jesus.'

The Laughter and the Hammer

My older brother and his friend
told me it was real:
a small creature with a stick
in its fist and a drum strapped
to its belly. It walked
along the workbench—I am not sure,
perhaps it stood still—beating
its drum. They said
it was a cricket. *Jiminy!*
they laughed
as they smashed it with a hammer.

For years afterwards
I kept a look out in the garden
knowing that only the sight of another
could atone for what I had seen.

Strange—even though I know
it was plastic, now—
how it still haunts me:
the cricket in its red tunic, like a soldier,
beating its drum;
the laughter and the hammer smashing down.

you know?

aiming
the can care
fully

i push the old
fashioned plunger
as my brother

places the lighted
match in front
of the nozzle

a puff of spray
a fuff of flame
the web disintegrates

and the spider
writhes
on the ground

who can stand
in the face of
technology?

what is left
if the old and new
combine?

of course
i do
the moral thing

and stepped on it—
we are not
barbarians

you know

Snake

The same as with men,
only less dangerously

the dugite

where the head goes
the body follows

The October Revolution

It came upon us like winter
after a long, long autumn,
stripped us of all our splendour,
chilled us to the very marrow of the brittle bone.

The land groaned with us in a great empathy.
The snow fell in a billion crosses
to sanctify the million souls soon to be lost.
The river's skin turned to steel.
The trees shed their clothes, stood naked
and dejected like huge skeletons,
jabbing their knuckles at the wind.

It was not long before we knew
that the sun would always hang, for us,
just below the black rim of the world.
Our skies put on the twilight like a uniform.
Our earth dressed in a sepia of grey—
without depth of shadow or distinction of light,
without bright of colour or sharp of shape.

We have become winter rivers
rigid on top, flowing always below
conforming to the dictates of our only season.

Yet still our hearts danced with joy
(and my voice almost dared to sing)
when the first Spring gushed upon the land.
A challenge to the commandments of the Movement!
A challenge beyond their control!
The sap shooting up to the sun,

bursting in salvoes of green!
The seeds flaring from the dank dark,
firing the fields with red and gold!

After Reading a Newspaper

It's as if some of the ink
that smudges my fingers
has blackened my soul, too.

I Whistle and They Come

The boy stands in the middle
of the painting, a tin whistle
in his mouth, a bucket of wheat
in his hand, and bantam hens
flocking to his feet,
stretching out their necks as they run.
And the painting's title extends
its loveliness: 'I Whistle and They Come.'

Why was it included in the selection?
There is no other like this one
among all the drawings in the collection
of *Pictures by Chinese Children*.
It alone does not trumpet or tell
the Foreword's claim that the children
'learn socialist cultural subjects well'.

'Let's All Criticise Lin Piao and Confucius'
suggests one drawing, with conscientious
children brandishing their small fists.
'The Army and the People Are One Family' insists
another. And a girl aged seven has drawn
a picture called 'Sparkling Red Stars'
of little children, all in uniform,
wearing army caps, and carrying spears.

'I Whistle and They Come'
is the only one, the only one
among all the paintings
that celebrates God's creation

without the slightest taint
of utility and indoctrination—
that says 'I', and does not assume
as absolute the 'we' of the commune.
This is a small triumph, then,
in the face of the darkest works of men.

And surely these other drawings
boast of dark things indeed.
They celebrate the ignoring
of every simple and lovely human need.
In each one, the seed
of self and personality,
of celebration and spontaneity,
has fallen on the sterile ground
of what some men perceive
and enforce as collective good.
How these children must grieve
over joys they have never understood!

And are the teachers proud
of what they have done?
Does their Party boast aloud:
We Whistle and They Come?

The Dogs
Concerning Cambodia

During the night the dogs came
and killed the bantam hens.
We heard nothing but the rain.

All night its tin refrain
smothered squawk and bark and din.
During the night the dogs came.

We find it hard to explain;
and where do we begin?
We heard nothing but the rain.

Perhaps the question is vain:
but were we asleep when,
during the night, the dogs came?

We live in the night's black bane:
we are sightless men.
We hear nothing but the rain.

And when they come again,
what will we say then?
During the night the dogs came
yet we heard nothing but the rain?

In Solidarity

for Lech Walesa and Solidarnosc – Poland, December 1981

We are the Socialist State:
our fist is an iron mace;
our heart is a pit of hate.

Hungary learnt too late
that freedom is fallen from grace.
We are the Socialist State.

We disavow Dubcek's mistake,
his fantasies of a 'human face'.
Our heart is a pit of hate.

Dare ten million workers debate
that History has hallowed our place?
We are the Socialist State!

We will crush Walesa the Ingrate
and the whole of the Polish race!
Our heart is a pit of hate.

Brothers, it is your fate
to fall to our embrace.
We are the Socialist State.
Our heart is a pit of hate.

Coda
We are the Socialist State.
Our good is your good,
though our means may seem malevolent
when our motives are misunderstood.

We are the Socialist State,
the Ultimate Good, and this is why
we will shoot the malcontent
who put in our mouths the lie:

Our heart is a pit of hate!

Election

Australia, 5 March 1983

On the weekend there was a change
of Government. New men with new motives
will make new laws
to maintain, mould and move us.

This morning, I drove through Perth
along Stirling Highway to Fremantle.
And I tell you this: I saw
no blood dried in the gutters,
no bodies strewn on the pavement,
no tanks stationed in the streets.
I swear: As usual, there were
girls in the malls,
cars on the carriageways,
ships in the port.

There is a new Government
but no one has gone
into hiding.

How the enslaved billions
must envy us! Without death or dread, we
changed our Government.

How it must flay them,
the Marxists and all the malevolent Ists,
to see the frieze of their tyrannies
illumined by the near-spent candle
of democracy.
Listen. I hear them
fumbling for the snuffers in the dark.

One Day

for Pedro Cruz

Deftly, the dragonfly
reconnoitres the polling station
Blitzing the flimsy booths, hovering
about the ballot boxes, it goes
unnoticed by voters, poll clerks
and the parties' snooping scrutineers.

With occult
precision, it pilots between obstacles,
disappears against the polished jarrah floor,
reappears in structured silhouette
against a dusty window.

Why has it strayed
to this dry bed of democracy?
It portends unremembered
but unbroken
alliances. *Caballito del diablo.*

When will the dragon
fly from our midst?

In between my duties (blue-pencilling
names from the Roll,
issuing ballot papers) I watch until
it disappears out the door.

Caballito del diablo: the devil's little horse.
One day it will return, bigger
and mounted with machine guns.

Not in Truce

Above the black soil of the bulldozed paddock
spiders have spun their threads
on upraised sticks and roots.
In the midst of anarchy, a small affirmation
of design. The webs,
wet with dew and infused with light,
are white pennants raised to proclaim
the mysterious endurance of the powerless.
Or they are bandages of fine gauze,
daubed where limbs have snapped, wrapped
to staunch the flow of beauty from the broken land.

And perhaps it's only little things that will remain
to shore the heart against the broad and brutal ugliness
that looms as the destiny of man. Perhaps
small gestures—the weaving of poems
or the pursuit of a personal integrity
or an unfaltering faith that God is good and
good is no illusion—are all that is left to us.
Like the spiders, we bind the broken roots.
Not in truce, but on trust, we raise
our ragged, regal flags in the winds of a desolate age.

I am Put in Mind of a Brave Man

Silence. A slight vibration,
a felt clacking
of the taut rubber
against the shaft of my sling
as I swim. Silence.
Over the sand, away
from the rockeries and rich greeneries of the reef.

Without warning, the cuttlefish-ribbed,
whiting-fish-white sand
planes in from every direction
to a crab—a large crab
clad in archaic armour
alarmed with outstretched arms.
Suddenly, a crab.
And I am put in mind of a brave man,
spirit raised to upbraid,
to embrace to the death
the clack of terror, the steel of tyranny.

Terror

Terror is multiform.

For the young chickens,
a new noise nearby
or a hawk in the clear sky
crushes them flat to the earth.

For each creature, terror
wears a different uniform.
For man, there are more
than the armies of the world.

For my small son, the neighbour's dog
is terror bounding towards him.
And before I can reach him, he falls
falls to the ground
in the sheer exultation
of fear. Hugging the hard earth
he screams for burial
as if in the tribulation.

Mowing

I turn to see my son behind me.
He pauses as I pause, a few paces
back in the swath in the weeds.

When did he leave the verandah?
When did he resolve the mower's roar
would no longer make him scream?

As I move off he comes on, ginger
as a cat. He is stalking his fear.
Come on, then, little one. Be brave.

Two isn't too young to rehearse.
Courage is hard, cowardice easy.
And fear … fear gets only worse.

The Servant

2 Kings 6

I awoke and walked out
and there they were:
the Syrians in their thousands
in their armour and in their chariots

Master! I called
I spoke and I awoke him
Master, I said (he arose and peered out)
What will we do?

Fear not, he said, and I
could not even muster laughter
Fear not, for those who are with us are more

I could have wept, I could have cursed:
this man of God is a fool to know no fear
Even if the king and his armies
had been with us here
at Dothan instead of Samaria
we still would have been as a little fish
before the jaws of leviathan

And then my master mumbled
as he often does
with his eyes clenched like fists
and his face towards the heavens

And suddenly I saw
a host, an army, a multitude round about me:
horses and chariots and warriors
beyond the mind's hope of counting

Stallions as white as the ocean's foam
and others of black and brindle and roan
stamping their feet in the mountains
striking their hooves like flint on the stone
champing at bits and tossing their heads
tossing and whinnying into the wind
their manes wimpling like banners
flowing out like fine samite
their eyes the fury of burning light
the brightness of broken coals

And the chariots!
Oh Lord, the chariots!
Of flame they were, of flame
all gold and vermilion and red
all yellow and gold and blue
licking and dancing into the heavens
dimming the very sun for brightness!
The rim of the world was afire with them!
I feared the vault of heaven would ignite
and the very mountains melt like lead!

And all the time the horses
snorting and pawing and pulling
urgent for battle
and the charioteers still and stern and unalarmed
awaiting a signal, a command

And to think and to think!
I was afraid of the Syrians,
of thousands of chariots of iron and wood
of soldiers of bone and blood!

The Woman Who Found the Well

John 4:1-39

Why, it was as if he lowered
a pail into the well of my soul
and brought it back brimming with secrets.
I told him things he already knew
because he first asked
of me a drink—I a Samaritan
and he a Jew.

Then *he* offered *me* a drink
said I should thirst
no more. I said
You have nothing
to draw with and
the well is deep.
But he repeated: Water
within you, welling up.

For a moment I mistook his meaning,
thought I'd not have to come
to this well again
in the dust and heat
after the other women had come and gone.

A Man Who Heard the Shepherd

John 10:11-16

and when
he called himself the shepherd of the flock
I thought straight away
of vipers

you know—how the shepherd
probes the field, pours pig's oil
around the vipers' holes
to imprison them
    —how the sheep
turn from the odour, keep
to pleasant pasture, ignorant
that a table is prepared for them
in the presence of enemies

oh I should have seen
no doubt
the oil of gladness
and the safety of the flock
but I confess I was caught
by the irony—pig's fat
staying the fangs of vipers!

The Children and the Dogs

Mark 7:24-30

We were at table when she came
uninvited into the room.
He saw her first. I looked up
and was furious. Always
the riff-raff. Other kings
retire to pomp and splendour
but He received only the praise
of the poor, was plagued
by petitions from the deformed
the diseased, the deranged:
'Son of David, have mercy!'
Have mercy! Can't He eat a meal
without their badgering?
I stood to deflect her
but she brushed past, making
my hands unclean. She was
a Gentile, as her garments
and bracelets betrayed. She said,
'Master, my daughter
has a devil. It makes her ill.'
A Gentile, a woman, a demon:
three in one, these filthy things
at my table. He dismissed her,
speaking as she spoke in Greek,
speaking as she could never speak
of the Covenant and the promises
to Israel. But she persisted,
which seemed to please Him
almost as much as it offended us.
He wiped a crust around the rim

of his bowl, gathering up
the gravy, and said, 'Should I
throw the children's bread
to the dogs?' I wanted to say
as the Romans say, 'Die, dog,
if you are not happy!' But
his manner restrained me.
There was a lightness, a love
about it. He was *bantering*
with her! I dare not judge
Jesus, but I must say I would
never play wits with a woman,
much less a *gentile* woman.
She replied, 'Yes, Lord, yet
even the whelps chance a crumb
while under the children's table.'
It was a winning riposte, mixing
cleverness with humility and faith.
He was impressed. He was moved.

Joseph of Arimathea
Luke 23:50-56

A bantam in a thorn bush;
vipers in the temple;
lamb's blood on the altar:
there were forebodings,
of course, but we never
expected this. His death
hollowed our hearts,
as if they were figs
from which the birds
had scooped the red flesh.

I had a hole in the hills
in readiness for my bones.
We approached the Governor
prepared to beg, but he
needed no persuasion.
He granted the body gladly,
eager to dip his bloody hands
into the basin of our request.

We lowered the cross,
puzzled how to prise
the nails from the wood
without further wounding
His ruined flesh. And all the while
His mother wailing
and the soldiers standing about.
At a loss, I lifted His head
and worked at the crown of thorns.
Then a soldier offered a suggestion.

At the tomb the women
wrapped his body in linen strips,
binding in the spices,
the aloes and myrrh
I had brought as the customary
pitiful stay to putrefaction.
Lastly, and in haste for dread
of the encroaching dark
and the defilement of the Sabbath,
they bandaged His head, covering
strip by stripe the features of His face—
one band for chin and lips,
one for nose and cheeks,
one band for eyes and eyebrows,
one for forehead—and then,
elliptical, from crown to chin,
several loops to cover the hair
and fasten at last around the throat.

When we'd done, the soldiers
hefted the stone into the doorway
and levered it flush with the butts
of their spears. Three walked
ahead of us into the twilight.
Two stayed behind on watch.

What they were guarding against
I could not guess. Neither stone
nor sentry were needed to keep Him in:
death, I thought, could do that alone.

Kangaroos

Silent as the light-
ly falling rain,
kangaroos are bounding
in single file
across the near paddock.

A buck, a doe, a joey,
diminishing in size
like a trick
of perspective, going
fast, their tails

working up and down
like the handle of a pump,
spring-loading
their legs for each jump.
Without pause, the buck

leaps the fence
but the smaller two balk
at the last moment.
Now, without momentum,
they are without hope

of hurdling the wire.
They race along the fence,
the curve of their down-
swinging tails touching
the angle of their up-

springing heels. It is
no use. The barrier
is unbroken. Finally
they stop, stand still
and stare into the bush.

Two grey skittle-shapes,
thalidomide paws
clasped to their chests.
Bewildered, they gaze back
across the open paddock

to where a rainbow has
raised a bright crosier
to bless the dreadful world.

Perhaps

Look, a parrot has carved
this gumnut with small curves
that touch sometimes to make
wings or, inverted, waves.

The bird, a rosella perhaps,
must have held the honkynut
in its claw and, hooking
its upper bill over the rim,

incised the green-glazed wood
with its lower bill. Perhaps
it found in the tree's living
pottery an object of beauty

and determined to decorate it
with a scalloped design.
Perhaps it has demonstrated
that creatures other than man

also have an aesthetic sense.
Or perhaps it simply found,
that rosella in this red gum,
a rather hard nut to crack.

Flag

On a towel on the line—
the shadow of a fairy wren,
its distinctive upright tail.

The towel a flag, now—
luxuriating in the breeze
with the emblem of a kingdom.

Robins in Stubble

i

The summer heat—
a pair of reckless robins
break the fire ban.

ii

Smouldering stubble—
suspicions abound about
the flamin' robins!

Touchy Stilt Tanka

1. Mismatch

If only you could,
dear dignified stilt, adjust
the length of your legs
to the depth of the water
in the diminishing dam!

2. Complaint

'Don't call me a *stilt*.
That's OBJECTIFICATION!
My legs are merely
one part of me,' complained Stilt,
otherwise known as Longshanks.

3. Features

That's the spirit, stilt!
Nothing can be done with those
laughably long legs
except make features of them.
Go on, colour them hot pink!

Ducks in the Rain

Four ducks are puddling about in the rain—
mongrel ducks, neither Muscovy nor Campbell,
mottled, fully feathered, but too young to sex.
Four recently-ducklings, the children's pets.

They step gingerly on the gravel, glance
quizzically at me through the study window.
I am, they know, harmless. *We have fouled
his doorstep*, they think, *and he has not shot us.*

He loves us. They are unquackingly confident.
They waddle in a huddle in the wet, the rain
rolling from their feathers like mercury.
With no thought for flight, one flaps wildly;

the others follow, stretching their necks,
standing on tiptoe. Like a gang of young women
(behold the bottoms!) up to no bad, they head
for the runoff that follows the raised edge

of the driveway, a shellac of swift water
no deeper than the webbing on their feet.
Stepping in, they imagine a river. They flatten
out, sleek themselves to the slick clay,

and scoot along the runnel like otters.
The grano's dream: a self-propelled trowel!
Imagine God's pleasure when He imagined
birds so decidedly ducky, so delightfully fowl!

Incarnation

It is an incarnation of an idea
from the mind of God, that robin

resting on the tomato stake
like a flame from Pentecost.

It is a modest manifestation
of His thought, His nature.

It is one small way I know
He is good, our God, our Creator.

Wire Wrens

i

Passing through yet
the wren pauses a moment
in the wire net.

ii

Just a set of hoops
for the wrens—the wire netting
of the chicken coop.

Imagining Wrens

Since the Creator
troubled to imagine wrens
I'm convinced it is
appropriate with my pen
to imagine them back again.

Zebra Finches, Station Country

i
A gust of finches
through the rails of the stockyard
to the drinking trough.

ii
Coming together
Brahmin cattle, zebra finches
to share the water.

iii
So very little—
the finches at the water trough
beside the cattle!

Hop

The grasshopper
beats the shutter …

Aha, but look
the pixels caught

the blur of legs,
the spurt of sand!

Remarkable
really—to miss

the grasshopper
but catch its hop!

Disturbance

Again from the corner
of my writing-room window

that sticky, ripping sound
as a plump spider scampers

in pursuit of some purpose
through and over its web—

that tacky, tearing sound
like Velcro unfastening.

Beachcombing

A leafy seadragon
washed ashore in the storm.

I pick it up, stare at
its miniature horse-head

drawn into a long snout
ending in 'O'. So sad,

that little mouth! O!
And yet as I walk on

with this treasure, I find
myself wishing the waves

would also wash ashore
a paper nautilus.

The Weight of the Baby

Marroning, Wellington Weir

I stay behind with the baby
while they check the baits—
my wife, my children. They are
that light skirting the shore.

My new son lounges in my arms,
staring at my face, which is
(like his own but less sweetly)
uneven with shadow and shine.

Gas hisses in the lamp's gauze.
A sudden wind scours the weir
like a scoop net. Behind me,
the trees break out in tongues.

Sensing the soft grasp of sleep,
the child begins to struggle,
limbs erratic and ineffectual
as a marron marooned on its back.

'Don't be cross,' I murmur,
hugging him, rocking him. 'Hush.'
I am gentled from my gender,
staying back with the baby.

He settles and slips away.
His head becomes heavy,
like a melon, in the crook
of my arm. Light meshes

in his hair as if in a mantle.
Distant but distinct, I hear
my eldest son scoop and exclaim.
A scrabble of claws on wire.

The water is black but the sky
is spattered with stars.
I imagine the many rubies
of the marron's torchlit eyes.

I watch my family, my loves,
move further into the darkness.
A mopoke cries from the forest.
I feel the weight of the baby.

I feel the weight but am light.
O Lord, my soul is very still,
quiet and still, even as an infant
asleep in his father's arms.

A Thing or Two about Monkeys

'There's no monkey in the shower,
see?' He is reluctant to look.
At two he's old enough to know
a thing or two about monkeys.

And there *is* one in the shower—
dangling, perhaps, from the nozzle,
waiting to drop on his head to
join the one causing the trouble.

But where did *that* one come from?
What word or image summoned it
to swing with grimace and gibber
through the synapses of his brain?

And how astonishing that it
could come at all! Can a monkey
imagine a boy in the shower?
So how then a boy, a monkey?

He peers into the tiled recess.
Is that a face behind the wash
cloth on the tap? Is that a paw
clasping the curtain to the rail?

He concedes at last his mistake.
But soon he begins to wonder,
Which rooms in the house are safe
now the monkey's left the shower?

Home
for Susan

The night is coming on fast now.
Looking out the window I see
the forest on the far hill
has become a mass of blackness
with frills against the skyline.
The kangaroos in the near paddock
have blurred into the pasture.
The irrigation dam down in the valley
glistens silver-grey, a scrap
of twilight torn from the sky.
The words I've been working with
are like running water. All afternoon
I've been trying to scoop out
a place for them to settle, a poem
where they can lie and reflect the light.
But it's too late now. The dark
is coming on fast, fast. And I want
to go home. My wife is expecting me.
She is in the kitchen right now
making tea, with the two little ones
tripping her up, climbing
over each other like ferrets.
She is waiting to ask me, 'How
did it go?' And I will say, 'Good.'
Or, 'Not so good.' Depending.
And she will kiss me, just a touch
of her lips to my lips, but
a touch nonetheless. And my sons,
with four years of life between them,
will bully me for attention.

And I will toss them about,
roughing them up with love.
And later tonight, before we join
the children in that no-place
of sleep, she might embrace me.
Or she might not. Either way
is fine. Tomorrow will be different.
Only her constancy is constant.
Two decades ago she vowed,
'With my body, my heart, my will,
I will.' And truly she has, does.
Amazing! My wife. She's the one,
she's the one I'm going home to now.
Home. The place she makes
by being there. The place
that resolves the question, 'Who,
who in this life will love me?'

The Grasshopper Heart

That man with the cowboy hat and tan and tattoos
is holding his little white-skinned daughter
very gently in the shallow water. Now he is
zooming her along, but not too quickly
for fear of her fear. He tosses her up,
catches and hugs her, holds in check
the fierce tenderness that craves to crush her.
Her father. His wholly holy love. He is smiling
and I know his heart is like a grasshopper—
leaping and landing spring-loaded to leap again.

That's Fish

Say 'Quark!' they say,
my daughters.

I comply.
And quick as casual

quoit players
they flick

their hands at me.
Inexplicable!

'That's fish,'
the elder explains.

Father, poet, pelican:
I am hungry

with happiness.
'Quark!'

They toss more
invisible fish.

Mirth with Meaning

After the meal, we read
the words of Christ in the Gospel
of Matthew: 'when you fast,
do not look dismal ... '

'What does "fast" mean?' I ask.
My daughter jumps from her chair
and races around the table.
'See—I'm fast!' she declares.

Who dares laugh? Angels
rollick about the room. I nod
earnestly. There is a smile
on the three Faces of God.

His Free Hand

On Robert Dickerson's oil painting, Lost Child

What to do with his free hand?
One hand cups her hip, holding
his arm like a rail at her back
to steady her on his left knee.

But his free hand, draped on
his uncommitted knee and almost
touching the hem of her frock
—his free hand is not free.

If she were his own, he would
run that hand over her shin,
feel the bird-like bone, knead
behind it the small soft calf.

Or in happiness he might perhaps
thump her chest with his palm
—or even, if she were his own,
brush with his knuckle her cheek.

But she is not his child, this
Lost Child, so he must comfort,
comfort her as best he can with
one hand, one knee, one heart.

Bereft, the small girl fingers
her fingers, her head resigned
to his shoulder, while he wonders
what to do with his free hand.

Art Gallery

Easy to succumb to idealism and elitism in this sanctuary.
Which is why the government has posted attendants, dressed up
like parking meter inspectors, within view of every painting.

They remind the romantic patron of the heart's disposition—
the thefts and desecrations that nap there with the nobler
sentiments art sometimes nudges awake. They are a reminder, too,

of the mundane. As the escalator delivers me to the floor
where the impressionists are hanging, I step between a male
and female attendant. As I get my bearings I overhear her

say to him, 'Have you ever tried those chicken sausages?'

The Sleep of the Upright

A man snared
by slumber

in a chair
in the library

has assumed
the pose of

a swan asleep—
neck curved,

head aslant
and down.

A gawky grace,
yet strangely moving—

for he looks
so vulnerable

without a wing
to cover his face.

Skittle

From the Craftsman's lathe,
a slender skittle—see
how from waist to hips
the young woman falls and flares!

Yet to the Maker's merriment
the skittle does the skittling—
see how she bowls over
every man who stares!

Threshold

She hesitates in the doorway of the cafe,
the young woman with milk in her breasts.

She stands against the light, her torso
tipped off-centre, her hip jutting out

to accommodate the child clasping her
blouse. She just stands at the threshold

as if she were not a miracle. At last
she steps into the dim room, strolls in,

the child straddling her hip, riding it
joyously, like a jockey on a victory lap.

Confinement

Bandyup Women's Prison

On the oblong of lawn
between the barred
walkway and the wall,
a young Malaysian woman

(straw hat held
against the slight wind,
free arm extended
for balance)

steps
sideways to avoid
the sprinkler's spray
in the confined space

lifts
astonishingly her feet
like an Andalusian horse
dancing.

Rain

A young Italian woman
in black
carrying groceries

And the rain
starting to fall

See how she bends
curls into herself
as if cowering
to avoid a blow

hurries along the footpath
huddling her parcels
to her breasts
for comfort
against the wind and the wet

Two Men

There are two men.
A man on the ground
is tossing bricks
to another on the scaffolding.

He swings each weight
in both hands
down to his knees
and up in a single movement.

How the bricks float up
to the catcher's hands …
like bubbles lifting
from the bottom of an aquarium!

Mr James

When I was a boy
and needed birds, Mr James
built a cage for me
from large pinewood cable-reels.

And at church on Sundays
he stood at the door,
crushed my knuckles
in the vice of his hand,

handed me a hymn book
from his brick-like stack
and banged me with the hammer
of his voice.

Of all the kind people
I have known in my life
this man is set apart,
having raised a cathedral in my heart.

The Worship Tanka

1. Psalm

The congregation,
singing David's ancient poem
to the mellow sound
of my daughter's saxophone:
so my soul longs after You ...

2. Benediction

For benediction
I raise my hand and the people
bow their heads—except
a small boy, who raises *his* hand
to bestow a blessing on *me*!

3. After Preaching

Thanking me warmly
for my sermon, an old woman—
'I couldn't hear it
myself, I'm nearly deaf, but
everyone said it was lovely.'

Pastor

Just after midnight
he calls from the hospital:
Oh, Andrew, my wife!
Who was it told me pastors
are out of touch with real life?

Plea

Peter or Thomas—
if not one, then the other
is my example.
Oh, my Master, have mercy
on me as you did on them!

Mixture

God is not so small
he must direct everything:
may not a leaf stir
without his finger's forcing?
Nor is he so big
he must neglect anything:
may not a leaf wave
as a sovereign beckoning?
So there's a mixture
in everything that happens
of management and freedom.

Path

If we look we see
the Son's light like the sun's light
makes a straight path
across the sea to each of us
wherever we stand on the shore.

Use

It is no excuse
and yet our sin has this use:
the Father of light
in the dark of our disgrace
shows the glory of his grace.

For Philip

This is what death has done:
Changed him beyond belief
Made him blind and dumb

Turned him cold to the sun
Blown him away like a leaf:
This is what death has done.

> Can a tune beat time
> On the drum of his ear
> Now silence is the sound
> That alone draws near?

Seeing his form, we are numb:
For whom did we make this wreath?
He is blind and dumb.

We huddle together as one,
Yet each alone in our grief.
This is what death has done.

> Can a maiden dance
> In the chamber of his heart
> Now his blood is still
> And he's set apart?

My mother mourns her son,
But tears are cold relief:
He is blind and dumb.

The words that twist my tongue
Are bitter beyond all grief:
Look what death has done—
Made him blind and dumb!

        Will the Day-Star rise
        To the circle of his sight?
        Will his tongue peal praise
        To the Father of Light?

Grief

It is nothing tangible, no action, no word that has been said,
Just a feeling that sweeps the soul quite without warning
As a wind brushes the growing grain briefly on a calm morning.
It is a grief, a sudden remembrance that he is dead.

It is a feeling and a fact that God alone may understand.
Though I strain to remember, I long to forget.
But neither gives refuge or relief: either holds sorrow and regret.
He is gone: the cup is broken, the water spilt upon the sand.

Like a haunted theatre, there are lights and sounds in my head.
My mind flicks through old film, jams on an almost forgotten frame:
I see his face, hear his voice—and mine, whispering his name.
And for a moment there is nothing, no one I would rather instead.

It dies quickly, lies lightly like an autumn leaf.
But who knows what winds may flick it up again, this grief?

Black Holes

Everywhere, death. In deep space
there are giant stars collapsed
into themselves, compressed
by their own weight.
As with a terrible grief,
their gravity is so great
not even light can escape.

It is hard to conceive:
black holes—voids
in the vacuum of space.

How long has it been
since the light left your face?
The heavens, my heart—
still I can't tell them apart.

I Do Not Forget

i

Sharing a dreadful purpose,
they arrived in the early morning—
my father and mother, my one remaining
brother—redeyed and riven with regret.

Philip is dead.

Death's ebony crook
hooked me
into the fold of grief.
Like sheep without a good shepherd
we huddled together.

ii

These days, when my father or mother
come to our home without warning,
I panic.

iii

He died while I slept.
Unknown to me, there was a moment
when the sweet and dreaming air
lapped into my lungs
but drained from his forever.
He died while I slept. Like a dream
he was gone when I awoke.

iv

Forever?

I believe
those who believe
share Christ's insurrection
against death.

Did he believe?

v

They wheeled the coffin
into the arctic room.

Like musk oxen,
we bunched together
to face the wolf of death.

vi

He lay dead in the coffin like a dead man.
Like a dead man he lay dead in the coffin.

vii

His right eyelid was slightly ajar
and death stared out at me
through the white of his eye.

viii

As we followed the heartblack hearse
I knew as never before:
Death is utterly perverse!

ix
At the graveside
I was appalled by apparitions
of decay.

x
After the funeral, we looked for photographs.

Like scavengers, my father and I
searched among his things
—picked through the flotsam
of his life, the debris
death had washed onto the shores of grief.

We found soiled snapshots
of his stereo, his dog—
but no picture of his face, nothing
to give relief.

We gave his stereo to the aimless
deathdazed youths
who shared his rented house.
I kept a photograph of the dog
leaping up at a hand
that might have been his.

At home, we rummaged
through drawers and albums—found him
strangely absent
from recent photographs of family
reunions and rituals—as if
our cameras had conspired with death
to efface even a record of his face.

xi

As Norsemen longed for ships
my brother pined for dogs.

I grieved for birds
and built cages. But our father
faltered at the prospect
of fluff on the carpet,
nip on the lawn. So Philip
was bereft of dogs
during his childhood days.

Long after the demon of his youth
had driven him from the family home
he was given a pup. It thrived
on his inarticulate love—
                    and died
in the car smash that killed him.

The Viking went down with his ship.

xii

I do not forget.

The Horseshoe Shooter

It is almost dark. A car passes
without its lights on. My son shoots it
with the hook end of his hockey stick.
'It shoots horseshoes,' he says.
I imagine a horseshoe
lobbing neatly onto the peg of the driver's neck.
'Piaow! Piaow!' cries my daughter,
improvising with her finger.
'Was this yours?' The old stick
is a new gift from his grandparents.
'No,' I say. 'It was my brother's.'
'Uncle David's?' My daughter is merely
revising the relationships: Dad's brother, my uncle.
'No. My brother Stephen. He's dead.'
They are both suddenly quiet. Their father
has a brother who is dead. Our father.
'Did you have any other brothers?'
'Yes. Philip.' 'Is he dead?' 'Yes.'
The horseshoe shooter has become a music stick
piping death from the basket of my life.
It rises up, the old snake, flicks
its forked tongue, flares its hood, sways, holds
them mesmerised. 'Were you grown up?'
They are thinking of each other now,
these little children, my son and daughter,
brother and sister. If Dad was a boy when …
are *we* safe? 'Yes,' I say.
Well, almost. 'Yes, I was grown up.'
They are relieved. But my daughter asks,
'And are you the oldest?'
'Well, I am now.' 'Good,' she says,

as if all uncertainties were now
settled, as if night were now the only darkness
coming upon the world. 'Good.'

Transience

i
This world of dew—
it's not illusion, it's the tears
we view it through.

ii
Christ will renew
all that is lovely about
this world of dew.

Even of Sky, Tree, Bird

'For we know that the whole creation groans and suffers ...' Romans 8:23

The light has painted,
as if with an air-brush,
ibis, wattle and cloud
on the river's canvas.

But just when you think
of naturalism, of photo-
realism—just when
you are about to exclaim,

'How exquisite, how nice!'
—just then the breeze
gives an expressionist
touch, distorts the lines

to reveal *The Scream*
at the heart of nature,
at the dear dumb heart
even of sky, tree, bird,

in this wounded world.

Suffering, Summer

If I'd remembered,
a little suffering could
have been averted—
if only I'd remembered
today to fill the birdbath.

Who?

The station owner
cordoned off the water trough
with sheets of steel mesh—
but who, I want to know, Who
festooned the mesh with finches?

Learning to Believe

Forget the hatchling altogether.
A whole chicken is too complex
by far. Faith, even blind faith,
must begin with something simpler.

Start with the egg-tooth fixed
to the tip of the bird's beak.
See it, that pinched flake of bone,
that tiny disposable barnacle?

Get a good look. Now, suspend
disbelief. Try to convince yourself
that Chance, abetted of course
by Time, invented that pick

and smuggled it to the prisoner.

Innocence

Little birds, I bet
it's fabulous not having
upfront to forget
yesterday before facing
a new day without regret.

Time

So much yet to do—
I must hurry, hurry up!
Even without theft
of a single one—I've still
fewer than forty years left!

Time to Write

i

Distracted by
the lack of distractions in
the empty house.

ii

A ream of paper—
I feel intimidated
just looking at it.

iii

I have waited
for weeks for the writing time
I have wasted.

Fruitless

Another day and still nothing
written. I deplore myself.
Of course, there's the family,
the phone, the worries. All
the ongoing things. This defence.

But truly mostly the day
was clear. A writer's dream
or nightmare. A free day.
And now a wasted day.
Squandered simply for lack

of discipline. A weakness
of will. No poem, no story,
no essay. No new sentence
in the novel. I am ashamed
of myself. Appalled. I recall

Jesus' parable of the fruitless
fig tree. Cut, cut it down,
the orchardist said. Why
should it use up the ground?
I have no answer, no reply.

Pain

Yesterday, when I woke early
with that pain and got up and got
no relief, I thought of death,
my death. This is it, I thought.

And I felt grief for my family
and friends. My two young sons
especially—fatherless in their
formative years. But mostly

I felt shame, an overwhelming
shame that I would soon meet
my Saviour with so little to give
in thanks. Inexcusably little.

Today the pain has gone, but
not the shame. Oh, dear Jesus!

The Turning

'It is not an enemy who taunts me—then I could bear it ...
But it is you, my equal, my companion, my familiar friend.' Psalm 55:12-13

Quick, so quick the turning
of the man who has turned
against me. To all who will
listen he says, 'He said this
and this.' Lord, you know.

Again and again he comes
against me with his mouth.
He tears, tears at my name.
He takes it in his teeth
and shakes it, like a hyena.

Yet have I not been to him
a pastor, a brother, a friend?
Oh, see how in his mouth
my name is all bloodied
with the blood of my heart!

Asking for Nothing

It has been a bad week.
A hard week. No time for joy.
My children? Who are they?
Those wildflowers outside
my window? I never noticed.

This morning, after the first
three phone calls, I left
my study for the bush.
I am sitting by a fire
smelling the aroma of burning

grasstree, hearing the billy
simmer, feeling the warmth.
I am asking for nothing
except escape. A bird
is singing too loud, as if

through a megaphone. A flame
flutters on a stick,
like a flag at half mast.
Just now, I opened the basket
my wife prepared for me.

There beside the coffee jar,
a packet of biscuits. The kind
I like. She has probably
been saving them for a day
like today, a day she knows

I need something sweet.

Two Words

Two lovely 'f' words
for newly weds and stayers
are 'fondle' and 'fond'.
For they fondle from fondness
and their fondling makes them fond.

Marriage
Genesis 26:8

Duty and delight
are one and the same in sex:
consider Isaac
reaching in for that softness
swelling in Rebecca's blouse.

You Gladly

for Susan

'The curves of your thighs
are like jewels, the work
of a skilled craftsman.' Who

did Solomon have in mind?
Dearest, I have you only,
you gladly, in mind. Re-

mind me again, won't you?
Allure me with the lines
and limber of your limbs.

As on our wedding night,
the first of all nights,
let me please the Craftsman

with my pleasure in you.

To Love and Life
A personal response to the International Conference
on Population Control, Cairo, September 1994

While delegates to the Cairo Conference
debated the merits of sterility and death

we took our clothes off, my wife and I,
and went to bed without a single barrier

to love and life. We felt *Oooh!* and *Oh!*
Thus blissfully our fifth child became.

Pathetic Things

*Concerning a protest against a Bill to legalise abortion
in Western Australia in May 1998*

What pathetic things we resort to
as we plead for the unborn children.

On the steps of Parliament House,
we have set out a thousand pairs

of bootees—one pair each for one tenth
of the babies aborted each year.

Two thousand empty bootees—blue,
pink—satin ribbon draw-strings

at their ankles to keep them on feet
that will never kick them off—

a visual lesson for the legislators
who will tomorrow pass a bill giving

'choice' to everyone but the child.
And so this display. It is pitiful,

pathetic! Don't think we don't
know it. But what else is left to us?

After protests, rallies, railings
and petitions, what else can we do

to turn the hearts of the heartless
from the homicide of the helpless?

The Same Mercy

After the legalisation of abortion in Western Australia in May 1998

When the Premier of Western Australia, Richard Court,
is finally tried for crimes against humanity

I'll come to his defence. I'll recall how courtly
he conducted himself in the low, low Lower House

two years short of the third millennium in the murky
month of May. I'll say, 'If it please the Court,

this honourable member, this premier politician,
should receive the same mercy he and his cohorts

gave to the unborn children in their abortion law
reform bill.' The bill the babies pay. Let the aborted

cry for justice, let the butchered bear a grudge.
I'll plead, 'Just the same measure of mercy, Oh Judge!'

Human Rights Poem for Christmas

Murder? I resent the implication!
It's hardly human. Take it from me—
all you see is blood. Get rid of it now.
Who would be the poorer?

Mary, I frankly don't believe
that angel-announcement stuff.
Nor will anyone else. Everyone
knows there's only one way ...

All right, calm down! The thing is,
you're not married. Think of the shame
once you begin to show. And Joseph ...
do you think he'll still want you?

Think of yourself, your future.
And think—they could stone you.
Then it would die anyway. Besides,
what sort of life will the little ... ?

Okay, Miss Still-a-Virgin, get off
your Son-of-the-Most-High horse!
I'm just trying to help. One day
you'll regret not listening to reason.

Reaction to a Retard

Disgusting, really, the way it disfigures
the face—a lack of intelligence. The retard
on the ferry has nothing going for him
except his mother, who gives him a regard

I struggle to comprehend. I hear a quick
voice cry, Better to kill him before birth!
I look at him and shudder at my own depravity.
How easy it is to deny a person worth—

to limit the human, which is the image
of God, to the beautiful and clever,
and to forget there is in every person
a spark, a spirit, that abides for ever.

There is a worse disorder than the damaged
brain that disfigures the blameless face.
It is the derangement of the cogent mind
that deforms the heart by a denial of grace.

Every Cell

While women try to leap it,
the gorge between the genders,
men mostly stand and gape.
Ah, that gorgeous otherness,
wider than ideology's lies!

Breast, larynx and brain,
hip, heart and thigh—every cell
in every part of every woman
is female, feminine, familiar-foreign—
every cell is chromosomed double-X.

O! No wonder men stagger
with attraction and astonishment,
all their cells and senses
calling, yearning, crying,
The second X is the reason Y!

Lighting a Match

She has learned at last to strike
the red end on the rough edge.
But still they break mid-stroke
or burn her fingers when they burst
to flame. Each match seems to provoke
a failure, invoke from her a cursed
performance. She has begun to learn
what some professors profess to spurn:
From literacy to love to lighting a match,
excellence is the objective ledge
onto which each labour must latch.
No charge of 'elitism' can hedge
this reality from our sight.
For even small things exact a pledge
that we shall do as they would like.

Learning the Language

CTA. How am I able to write
even this? For, in the beginning,
there is a supposition that I know
the letters and their correlation
by the rules of language to 'it'.
TCA. 'It' is in my children's sandpit
scratching a hole for 'its' excrement.
ATC? This is a question of excellence.
A partaking of a perfection. WAAAOW!
my daughter squeals, finding her sound
to signify the thing whose existence
excites her. We mimic her, charmed
by her childishness. Were she older,
it would be grotesque, this word-
lessness. TAC. 'It' squats in the sand,
tail twitching. Our language—has it
no objective reality? Are standards
in literacy and literature really
illusory, elitist? ACT. Scat!
'It' leaps from the sandpit, scrabbles
over the picket fence. (How can I say
these things, how can you receive them,
if not in obedience to something Other?)
WAAAOW! Soon my daughter will conform
to the conventions that will liberate
her into speech. She will learn most
excellently to say, Pussy. CAT.

Like Stephen

Stephen my son, you are
four before my heart is ready.

How quickly you quit yourself!
Well then, if you must

lose your winsomeways
may you win wisdom

and (like Spiritfilled, stonefelled
Stephen) may you be veryvaliant

in our Saviour's service.

Ronin

The samurai
regarded it loss and disgrace
to be lordless.
They vested pride and purpose in
loyal service.
Yet men today rebel against
the best of lords,
choosing to be ronin, wave men,
pitching on the whims of passion.

Samurai

Like the samurai
I long not to shame myself
or my Lord in death.
Yet those ancient warriors
are beyond compare
in bare courage and resolve.
I fear I'll never
match such mighty ones as them.
Yet my Lord avers:
Not your courage but my grace
will defend you from disgrace.

Illusion

This ailing world
is not an illusion, but
an illustration
of the ills our illusions and
delusions have occasioned.

Matter

It wouldn't matter
whether I'm merely matter
but for this matter
of the achings that matter
to the part that's not matter.

Touch

When I touched him, the old man,
when I interrupted his struggle
to remember what he wanted
to say and said, 'Look

at the rainbow bird'—
when I touched his arm
the flesh was saggy, loose
like old canvas on a windless day.

I tried not to think of it.
I let go and said, 'Up there,
look.' It was on the high wire,
colourless against the clear sky.

No hint of iridescence,
no hues of rainbows, but
I recognised its shape—
the bullet body, the sharp beak,

the twin thin feathers
trailing from the tail.
He looked up, the old man
looked up and looked puzzled.

'I used to know all the names,'
he said. 'What did you call it?'
'A rainbow bird. They come down
from the Kimberley to nest.'

'I love birds. I used to know
all the names. But now
I don't know any.' This horror.
The mind like the arm and

a greater slackness coming.
When I looked back, the bird
was gone. Only the wire
like a scratch on the perfect sky.

Bravery

When I face the grave
Jesus will not deplore me
if I am not brave.
After all, it was hardly
a strong man he came to save.

Dignity

To be dignified
when facing death is mainly
a matter of pride.
What matters most is to trust
the One who was crucified.

Time Zone, Sydney

Perhaps she is out of kilter,
being in another time zone.
Perhaps she would never do this
at home, surrounded by her own

people, possessions and purpose.
But here she is in the window
of the Timezone video game
store, unable to win or go.

She is playing the Skill Tester
machine, trying to win a toy
for the cost of twenty cents.
It's plain the machine is a ploy

to catch the small-time gambler,
pinch his wallet or her purse.
Now this Japanese grandmother
feels the Something-for-Nothing curse.

The toys are fluffy, bright and cute
(would you like a rabbit or a bear?),
the sort of knick-knack you could win
at darts at any country fair.

Barely worth a dollar, each toy
conjures thoughts of children, makes
even men maternal. What small child
is in this woman's mind as she takes

another coin from her purse, slips
it in the slot and sets the crane
in motion? She manoeuvres the three-
pronged claw over the bear again.

The talon drops, clasps the teddy
by its head, and lifts. But the prongs
lack the power to grip the few grams
of fluff. It's like using salad tongs

to lift a brick. The bear barely
budges from its nestled spot.
She is distressed. She knows it is
a sham, and yet she cannot stop.

Not hope but futility now
drives her on. To have spent so much
and still not have a prize! She works
the claw that has her in its clutch.

Woman Weeping, Sydney

Because she is sitting side-on to me,
I can see she has been crying, the woman
wearing mirrored glasses in the cafe.

Pity the animals, that they cannot weep.
Pity us, that we can, must, so often.
Her boyfriend returns with ice coffees.

She glances at him with her hidden eyes.
Her face crumples a little, sucked in
by the vacuum of her grief. He offers

a paper napkin, and she dabs her eyes,
shunting her sunglasses up the bridge
of her nose. Then she clears the mucus.

He looks away as one looks away from
something unpleasant. Shoring her face
with an unsure smile, she sips her coffee,

her larynx almost jamming in her throat.
He takes a tourist map from his backpack,
lays it between them, studies the streets.

She parts her thin lips, making a path
to her lungs for the persistent air.
She says something to him. Foreign words.

What is the meaning? Why is she crying?
Has he hurt her? Is she ill? Homesick?
Surely, she is far from home. Very far.

We all are. Only most of us don't know it.

Scotsman in Sydney

A man is playing the bagpipe
beneath the railway bridge
beside Circular Quay. No one
is listening. No one but me.

His face is as red as the cloth
on the bag of his pipes.
He fills his chest, his cheeks,
the bag. And the bag fills

the air with a high, haunting
sound—a melody undaunted
by the intermittent roar
of the trains and the constant

drone of the traffic. A tune
from a far country and a far
century but familiar just
the same. The unchanging heart.

I am in my own country but
I am far from home. Now
this Scotsman has betrayed me
to loneliness and longing

with his sweet, whining song.

Healing

I

There comes a time when longing fills the soul.
Shapes lose their power on the mind
and to the bright of colour the eye is blind.
Strangely, without warning, we are no longer whole
and all things are gone beyond our control.
In the subtlety of sound the ear can find
no euphony; and the heart, inclined
to sadness, in everything finds nothing to extol.

It is as if too long and too far from home
we have journeyed without thinking
of arrival—and standing finally alone
at the water's edge with the last light winking,
we find all things tinged with tragedy,
like the sun sinking down to the sea.

II

The sun sinking down to the sea,
magenta and majestic in his splendour,
appears powerless to prevent the plunder
of night. *Rise up! Look on us and let us see!*
But he is gone. Will he ever again be free?
He stood for a moment on the water
then was swallowed up, seemingly forever.
Who are we to have seen this? Oh, who are we?

Yet still we stand in the darkness waiting
for something to happen, for something more.
The moon is ill and the stars fall fainting
while the waves wash muted on our shore.
The brush of night tars the troubled air
and the heart's longing turns to despair.

III

The heart's longing turns to despair
and all seems dark and death within.
Yet in the din of defeat the voice of victory rings,
peals out the promise of our Creator's care.
There begins in our being the flare
of dawn: the Sun rising with healing in his wings.
With the gold of his blood he spins
fine silk, weaves a mantle for the faint to wear.

All things again are new and bright,
from the great to the least, the comely to the plain,
each in its own way is clothed with light.
In passing loss is permanent gain.
Hence, that if it will it might be whole,
there comes a time when longing fills the soul.

Boat

The new boat. I bought it mostly
for my boy, who at fifteen has become
black and thunderous. An aluminium
dinghy with ten horses behind it—
something to interest him, something
to give us something in common.
And yesterday it did. I swear
he was almost happy as we launched
the boat in the bay for the first time.
Our small craft. At full throttle
it sat up and planed! A sensation
of speed, as in a go-kart! Today
he wants to try it by himself.
Sure, I say, stepping to the shore.
Why not? I push the prow out to sea.
He pulls the cord and powers away,
heads out without looking back.
The dinghy skips over the light chop,
going out and out. I watch him,
the boy I've not loved nearly enough.
My son, who grows bigger in my heart
even as he grows smaller in my eyes.
He is on the sea, going directly
away from me. And I notice now
what I should have noticed before—
the cloudbank on the horizon.
Black clouds coming in. And the boy
still going out! I watch and watch,
willing him to turn. The boat
no longer glints, having gone
into the shadow of the clouds.

Then suddenly a tear, a bright tear
in the fast encroaching blackness.
And another. No thunder. No rain.
Just lightning, synapsing the dark sky
to the dark sea! The level sea,
on which my son is the highest point.
The empty sea, on which our boat
is the only boat. Lightning! Oh son,
turn back, turn back to the shore!
I beckon and call. But he has gone
too far to see or hear me any more.

Discoveries

'For the Spirit searches everything,
even the depths of God.' 1 Corinthians 2:10

Searching the divine depths,
the Spirit said, 'Ah-ha!
A sun, a tree, a man! Look!'

And the Father, delighted,
said, 'Certainly! Why not?'
He said, 'Home-of-my-heart,
look, would you like them?'

And the Son said, 'Yes. All
of them. The lions, lilies
and sparrows, too. But most
of all, the man, the woman.'

The Spirit, still searching,
cried, 'Aaah! Filth and pain!
I see nails and a hammer!'

The Son replied, 'Nonetheless,
I will be satisfied.'

And the Father, grieved,
said, 'Oh, Heart-of-my-joy,
we will show ourself glorious,
glorious in grace in you.'

And they Three as One
said, 'Let there be light,
and a garden!'

White Ibis

It is luminous,
the ibis standing
on the shimmer
of its reflection
in the autumn light.

The water lilies
defer to it.
The breeze touches
reverently the hem
of its garment.

Spreading its wings,
it adorns the sky
as a seraph
adorns with adoration
the eternal heavens.

Breaking free from
the departing bird,
a single feather
shies and spins
in the wings' wake.

Alighting, the plume
lies like foam
on the restless
water, a token
of something numinous.

Beliefs about Ibises

Although they weren't right,
they were on the right track,
those ancient Egyptians.

White ibises are indeed sacred,
not because they are gods, but
because they are intimations

of God—the invisible God
by whom and in whom 'we live
and move and have our being.'

How much closer to the truth
they were than modern men—
men who scoff at the sacred,

believing in their disbelief
that ibises were once lizards,
their feathers once scales!

That Colour

The crimson flowers
of the mesembryanthemum
by the roadside

burr like a skid mark.
Even when you stop
the car the colour

keeps hurtling
off to glory.
That colour is so

bright, so luminous,
it knocks your eyes
out of focus.

It's so boisterous
even God
couldn't keep it

within the lines
when He painted
the slender petals.

Petal Haiku

i

May or may not
have a tinge of pink—single
almond petal.

ii

The same angle—
the random almond petals
in the slight breeze.

iii

Fallen together
the near-white almond petals
blushing a little.

iv

Preventing me
from mowing, the pale petals
of the almond.

Apple Tree

for Susan

I am won and wounded by
the apparition of the apple tree
beneath the black sky:

a thousand leaves shifting
singularly in the one wind,
and the white petals sifting

to the dark and dunged loam.
Tell me, lady: In my absence
has our apple come into bloom?

And have the petals fallen to your hair
as once last summer
I saw them fall and snare?

Counterpoise

Light refracting on the reach of the river;
gulls and sails embracing the slight wind;
jellyfish clasping the calm water
or bunting the sand in the basking shallows;
posts of wood barnacled and rotten;
small waves lisping upon the shore:
here is an opulence I had forgotten.

And here and there, a scatter of children
scamper across the lawn like leaves
driven before the tempest of their happiness.
Parents and grandparents are at ease
in the shade of trees and in each other's company.
For these people, things I thought we had lost
have never been open to doubt.

As the sun departs, parties arrive for prawning:
light their lanterns and lay out their nets.
The world again seems young and lovely,
values certain and strong: young men
and old men, friends, fathers and sons
in pairs dissolve into the dark water
and toil together in the hope of harvest.

How ignorant I have been
through these last years of learning,
how weighted down on one side of the scale.
The large, deep things are all
in their own ways dark and hard.
Small things are a counterpoise
to lighten and soften the heart.

Fire From Dark Water

By the far shore, the lights
are bright oils on a black canvas.
In the still night, voices ring
round the rim of the river: men confess

friendship, baptised in common purpose.
The moon is a sickle in a field of wheat.
So much is ripe for harvest!
The wind stirring, my soul is replete

with image and reflection.
There is time for gladness, time to forget
time. It is more than prawns
we will catch with this net.

Garfish scud, prawns skip as we approach.
Between us the net is aglow
like the mantle of a lamp.
How much loveliness can one man know?

Look—such luminescence! I stamp
my foot. My legs are trees, burning, a bark
of bright coal. Each step
is a strong wind, a flaying of sparks.

So, fire breaking from dark water
along the river, within our hearts.

For the Force of Flame

For the force of flame, a thousand voices shout:
in the moment of change, each leaf cries out,
leaps up redly, brightly eclipsing the white
stars, before flickering and fading into night.

The moon is a water-smoothed stone on a riverbed,
shimmering beneath the streaming smoke. The crack and cough
of coals counterpoint the flames' stutter. Strangely enough
I remember the voice of the fire, but not the things we said.

We re-affirmed what we already knew: we do not agree on this,
on that. How foolishly we darkened simple pleasures—
friendship, fire, roast potatoes and fish—
with our convoluted talk. Life has its proportions and measures:

I would learn them before my soul cries out to its Creator,
leaps, stuttering with joy and shame, up to my Saviour.

Flying Home

That long moment of almost-panic
as the aeroplane accelerates along the runway
and leaves the ground—no longer

touches its shadow. We are airborne.
The wheels thump into the undercarriage
and the wing at my window swings up

lazily, like the great glorious flipper
of a whale rolling in the water. We climb
through the dark clouds into the sunlight

the city has not seen for days. And still
we rise, far above the canopies of the cumuli
until we level at eleven thousand metres.

Try not to think of it: eleven kilometres
to fall. We are flying west against the east-
ward spinning earth. The low sun

will be slow setting for us. I glance
down at the cloudscape, irregular as pack ice.
Gliding smoothly over the surface,

keeping pace with the plane, I see
a rainbow—round as a halo, and radiant.
A seven-coloured circle with a shadow

at its centre. We are a dark spot
in a nimbus, a flaw at the heart of a cut
and polished stone. And yet

it is our fuselage that is the focus
for the concentric colours. Indigo, yellow, red:
the rainbow enfolds us like a promise.

Homecoming
for Susan

Strange, this disturbance ...
drawn to the window again ...
and there you are, framed
by the world, walking alone
along the street, coming home.

Sonnet of Thanksgiving

I wake, draw the curtains and am suddenly aware
that He is profligate, our God, giving us more
than we need, more than we ever dream to ask for.
Through the window on this winter morning, there

beside my house, the forest is faint with mist.
The white trees are like women standing half-seen
in a sauna. The bushes where the spiders have been
are strewn with ornaments for throat and wrist:

necklaces, bracelets strung with diamonds. A stark
and startling wealth, this jewellery the women
have put off. They stand in silent communion:
unadorned, white, bar the occasional birthmark.

And then in the stillness, the whiteness, the swirl,
a lone bird call. It hangs on the ear like a pearl.

Light

Outside, a ceiling of off-white clouds.
Yet this cafe is spacious with light.
Not streaming in. Rather, a diffusion.

I am sitting where the uncurtained windows
of two walls meet. The light is light
about me. There are pansies on the table,

a bright posy on the blond pinewood.
Such a skilful arrangement of light—
yellow, mauve, white—each glad flower

splitting or splicing the spectrum
into voluptuous petal shapes. Pansies.
Flowers a woman lifts to her nose,

not simply for the scent, but for the cool
velvety touch. Flowers that belong
in a woman's hair, as a ribbon belongs.

A smiling woman brings my coffee, a doily
in the saucer. And, as a kindness,
two chocolates freckled with 100s & 1000s—

red, yellow, mauve, white. I stir sugar
into the coffee. The chocolates are sweet.
In fact, it is all sweet, all luminous,

all in accord with the Father of Lights
from whom all blessings flow
and in whom is no shift or shadow.

Perspective

I am in the Gentlemen's in a hotel
in George Street, combing my hair
after a shower. The tines of the comb
pleasantly scarify my scalp.
I am not this moment missing home.

I am standing in the glass when
something shatters. The door bursts back
and a middle-aged man storms in
like the Gestapo. But his attire arrests
alarm: pyjama pants, a towel on

his shoulder like a toga. He grins
at me. 'It's jolly amazing!'
he says. I laugh and shake my head.
Yes. Yes, it is. I plainly know it
now—now that it has been said.

Amazing! I collect my things: soap,
sodden towel, toothbrush. I hear
the water spurt against his skin.
And as I leave he begins to sing—
great gusts of sound as loud as his grin.

Suddenly Gladdened

My son, intent on cars and Lego.
Chancing upon him, I stoop
to touch his head—not a one-handed
tousling, but a two-handed clasping.

Sometimes a father must do this
to a just-five son. Sometimes
the heart presses the hands to worship
at the temples. Without insolence,

he ignores me. They are, he knows,
a hazard of childhood—Hug Interruptions.
So tedious, especially hand-head hugs
when you're trying to do Something.

Ho hum. *Brrr-um! Dad loves me.*
That insouciant head, these intrusive
hands! I move on, suddenly gladdened
my love has been taken for granted.

Grace

It is the genuflexion of the head,
whether tonsured or permed,
that believers have thrice-daily
in common. A communion of thanksgiving.

'For what we are about to receive ...'
So easy to make of it a mockery
or a cliché. And yet these words,
or the gist of them, hold a real if ritual
gratitude. Or a sadness at the discrepancy
between what is and what ought to be.
'... Lord, make us truly thankful.'

Monks in the refectory, mothers
in the kitchen, give thanks before
the first mouthful of every meal.

In the labour and re-education camps
maimed men and wasted women
murmur without a mutter before
guzzling their gruel. In the black lands
where droughts and dictators conspire
against the belly, believers still
say the blessing as they apportion
the last cup of begged grain.

Others, in the wonderworld of the West,
are flustered as they bow at their feasts
by memories of the dreams of Joseph:
the lean cows eating up the sleek ones—
the famished beasts coming out of the river

dripping and treading down the reeds
and eating their kind, their kith and kine,
like cannibals. The bellows. The blood
on the bovine teeth. And the second dream
of the seven fat ears of wheat
eaten up by the seven skinny. Horrible,
the blighted grain gaping ravenously.
A nightmare. Let those who have ears hear.

Yet without ears, He hears.
Our infinite, intimate God leans to listen
to the myriad momentary prayers
of His people. Saying grace. It is our incense.
It is, beyond explanation, His satisfaction.

'Let us give thanks.' And millions
at mealtimes do. Even infants,
those most insouciant of souls,
offer thanksgiving with cries and cooing
as they nuzzle at the breast—
that guzzle-and-come-again fount
where form and feast fuse in bliss
and soft blessing. See how they tug
away from the nipple, smiling.

Eyes closed and heads bowed: It is
the only way to look up. Thank
You. And think of it, the dignity
we gain through humility. Being
grateful. Giving thanks. That precious
repetitious prayer that makes us remember
grace as we say it.

THE GOD OF THE GLIMPSES:
A SEQUENCE OF POEMS ON THE PROPHET ELIJAH

And Omri slept with his fathers and was buried in Samaria, and Ahab his son reigned in his place. In the thirty-eighth year of Asa king of Judah, Ahab the son of Omri began to reign over Israel, and Ahab the son of Omri reigned over Israel in Samaria twenty-two years. And Ahab the son of Omri did evil in the sight of the LORD, more than all who were before him. And as if it had been a light thing for him to walk in the sins of Jeroboam the son of Nebat, he took for his wife Jezebel the daughter of Ethbaal king of the Sidonians, and went and served Baal and worshiped him. He erected an altar for Baal in the house of Baal, which he built in Samaria. And Ahab made an Asherah. Ahab did more to provoke the LORD, the God of Israel, to anger than all the kings of Israel who were before him. In his days Hiel of Bethel built Jericho. He laid its foundation at the cost of Abiram his firstborn, and set up its gates at the cost of his youngest son Segub, according to the word of the LORD, which he spoke by Joshua the son of Nun. Now Elijah the Tishbite, of Tishbe in Gilead, said to Ahab, 'As the LORD the God of Israel lives, before whom I stand, there shall be neither dew nor rain these years, except by my word.' And the word of the LORD came to him, 'Depart from here and turn eastward and hide yourself by the brook Cherith, which is east of the Jordan. You shall drink from the brook, and I have commanded the ravens to feed you there.' So he went and did according to the word of the LORD. He went and lived by the brook Cherith that is east of the Jordan. And the ravens brought him bread and meat in the morning, and bread and meat in the evening, and he drank from the brook. And after a while the brook dried up, because there was no rain in the land. Then the word of the LORD came to him, 'Arise, go to Zarephath, which belongs to Sidon, and dwell there. Behold, I have commanded a widow there to feed you.' So he arose and went to Zarephath. And when he came to the gate of the city, behold, a widow was there gathering sticks. And he called to her and said, 'Bring me a little water in a vessel, that I may drink.' And as she was going to bring it, he called to her and said, 'Bring me a morsel of bread in your hand.' And she said, 'As the LORD your God lives, I have nothing baked, only a handful of flour in a jar and a little oil in a jug. And now I am gathering a couple of sticks that I may go in and prepare it for myself and my son, that we may eat it and die.' And Elijah said to her, 'Do not fear; go and do as you have said. But first make me a little cake of it and bring it to me, and afterward make something for yourself and your son. For thus says the LORD the God of Israel, 'The jar of flour shall not be spent, and the jug of oil shall not be empty, until the day that the LORD sends rain upon the earth." And she went and did as Elijah said. And she and he and her household ate for many days. The jar of flour was not spent, neither did the jug of oil become empty, according to the word of the LORD that he spoke by Elijah. After this the son of the woman, the mistress of the house, became ill. And his illness was so severe that there was no breath left in him. And she said to Elijah, 'What have you against me, O man of God? You have come to me to bring my sin to remembrance and to cause the death of my son!' And he said to her, 'Give me your son.' And he took him from her arms and carried him up into the upper chamber where he lodged, and laid him on his own bed. And he cried to the LORD, 'O LORD my God, have you brought calamity even upon the widow with whom I sojourn, by killing her son?' Then he stretched himself upon the child three times and cried to the LORD, 'O LORD my God, let this child's life come into him again.' And the LORD listened to the voice of Elijah. And the life of the child came into him again, and he revived. And Elijah took the child and brought him down from the upper chamber into the house and delivered him to his mother. And Elijah said, 'See, your son lives.' And the woman said to Elijah, 'Now I know that you are a man of God, and that the word of the LORD in your mouth is truth.' After many days the word of the LORD came to Elijah, in the third year, saying, 'Go, show yourself to Ahab, and I will send rain upon the earth.' So Elijah went to show himself to Ahab. Now the famine was severe in Samaria. And Ahab called Obadiah, who was over the household. (Now Obadiah feared the LORD greatly, and when Jezebel cut off the prophets of the LORD, Obadiah took a hundred prophets and hid them by fifties in a cave and fed them with bread and water.) And Ahab said to Obadiah, 'Go through the land to all the springs of water and to all the valleys. Perhaps we may find grass and save the horses and mules alive, and not lose some of the animals.' So they divided the land between them to pass through it. Ahab went in one direction by himself, and Obadiah went in another direction by himself. And as Obadiah was on the way, behold, Elijah met him. And Obadiah recognized him and fell on his face and said, 'Is it you, my lord Elijah?' And he answered him, 'It is I. Go, tell your lord, "Behold, Elijah is here."' And he said, 'How have I sinned, that you would give your servant into the hand of Ahab, to kill me? As the LORD your God lives, there is no nation or kingdom where my lord has not sent to seek you. And when they would say, "He is not here," he would take an oath of the kingdom or nation, that they had not found you. And now you say, "Go, tell your lord, 'Behold, Elijah is here.'"'

The Holy Bible, 1 Kings 16:28-18:11

(tr. English Standard Version)

i. Ahab

My Gifts to Jezebel

As is the custom when a king marries outside
his kingdom, I provided for my wife's worship.
I built a temple for Melquart, one of the gods
we call 'Baal', in my capital, Samaria, close
to the palace. She was pleased but
not well enough. On the day of dedication,
while the bull's blood was still steaming
on the altar, she took me aside and wrapped
herself around me (oh, how my blood
hammers at the barest remembrance of it!)
and whispered hotly, 'Would you make a eunuch
of Melquart? Would you deny him this?' And so
I knew I must make a holy place for his consort,
for Asherah, the Lady of the Sea, the goddess
of war and sex. I sent to Phoenicia,
to the cities of Sidon and Tyre, for craftsmen
and they came and carved the goddess from wood
they had brought for the purpose. Asherah,
crowned with three horns, sitting astride
a lion, her breasts abreast of its mane,
a lily in her right hand for loveliness
and lust, the serpent of fertility in her left.
And they set her between the stone pillars
and the altars of incense, and planted
a grove of trees to mark the circumference
of the hallowed ground. And after the craftsmen
came the *qedishim*, the sodomites, who serve
the patrons of the shrine—the male
cult prostitutes, a gift from my father-in-law,
Ethbaal, king of two cities, priest of two gods.

As for the *qedeshoth*, the sacred harlots,
I gave up my concubines at the queen's request.
The temple of Baal, the grove of Asherah:
these are my gifts to Jezebel, my queen.
There are rumours that I am not a believer.
Perhaps. Yet I go up to worship,
that is certain. Some say I do this to content
the queen. I do not deny it. I say it plainly:
my acquiescence is her aphrodisiac.
She pleases me when she is pleased with me
and for her pleasure I'll pay any price.

ii. Elijah

When the News Came

I was in Gilead, fording the River Jabbok,
when the news came that the king had married
a princess of the Phoenicians, to make her,
a heathen, queen over the Northern Kingdom.
And I learnt also that the king had built
a temple to Baal, the no-god of the Phoenicians.
And I was in Gilead, sacrificing a lamb
on the altar at Penuel, where Jacob wrestled
with Yahweh for a new name, 'Israel',
when news came that the king had made an Asherah
in a high place above Samaria, with chambers
for her prostitutes. And I learnt that Jezebel,
our queen, had slaughtered some of the prophets
of Yahweh, offering their blood as an oblation
to the goddess at the dedication of her temple.
And I was in distress when I heard these things.
So I turned to the Sacred Scrolls and read them
day and night. And I read the commandments Yahweh
had written upon the tablets of stone: 'You shall
have no other gods before me.' Then I prayed
that I might know what to do. And I read
the warning in the Law of Moses, 'Take heed
lest your heart be deceived, and you turn aside
and serve other gods and worship them,
and the anger of the Lord be kindled against you,
and he shut up the heavens, so that there be
no rain.' Then I prayed fervently because I knew
what to pray. And I prayed fearfully because
I knew what to do. So I set off for Samaria,
praying that God would perform His promise

and preserve His servant in the performance.
I approached the throne and said to the king,
'As the Lord the God of Israel lives, no rain shall fall.'

iii. Elijah

Before Whom I Stand

Ahab's sceptre became a throwing-club
but I dodged it and declared again,
'The Lord, before whom I stand,
has given even the dew to my command.'
'Before whom you stand? You stand
before *me*,' he raged, standing, 'and I will
stand you no longer! Go back, back
to Gilead, to the goats whose hair and stink
you wear. Go back to Bethel and tell
the prophets, 'The king says, "Beware!"''
Then Jezebel fixed me with her painted eyes,
her impassive face. Hard as sling-stones,
her eyes in their pouches of paint. 'Tishbite,'
she said. 'Beware.' Cold as a blade
in the beating heart, her heartless voice.
Did I wince? Did I reel? Truly, it is monstrous,
that blend of malice and beauty
in the person of her Majesty! I turned my back,
turned to quit the perfume and perfidy
of the court, and that instant I imagined
a javelin flying from Jezebel's hand
to find a joint in the notches of my spine.

iv. Jezebel

The God of the Storms

When the prophet of Yahweh said, 'No rain
but by my word,' I summoned the prophets
of Baal, my prophets, and said, 'Pray
to Baal, the god of the storms and seasons.
Pray for rain.' Elijah is but one man
and Yahweh is but one god. My prophets
are many and Baal is mighty. I commanded
my prophets, 'Pray!' And they began.
I can hear them in the temple, the four
hundred and fifty voices chanting as one
voice. Soon Baal will answer with thunder.

v. Elijah

On the Way

As bidden, I set out for the Brook Cherith,
that small wadi I once waded
in the highs of childhood in the hills of Gilead.
And as I made my way, I saw a maiden
kneeling at her quern, grinding grain.
Her head was uncovered and her hair
fell forward to her face like a veil.
I asked her to bake me a scone
but she sent me away with scorn.
It was hot. Already the land was parched.
I trudged on and saw a man ploughing
with an ox and an ass yoked together,
contrary to the commandments. I stumbled
across the broken ground, following
his furrow until I caught him,
and confronted him with his crime.
He said, 'Father, I am poor.
I have one ass. I had two oxen
but one is dead. Should one beast
bear the burden alone?' Oh Lord!
Should one bear the burden alone?
I did not stop to argue. I said,
'Remember the Law, remember the purity
of Israel.' The dust of his work
engulfed me as I walked away. Then,
as if the seasons and their appropriate
labours had broken their appointed
boundaries, I saw a youth driving
four oxen over his barley. Four oxen,
sixteen hooves treading out the grain

on the threshing-floor of his fathers.
Bent with my own burdens, I barely
noticed that the beasts were muzzled,
their mouths enmeshed in nets of rope.
When men turn from truth, even the beasts
suffer. He smiled as I passed. Ignorant
of the Law, how could he be ashamed
of breaking it? Surely the king
and his consort will account for this!
As I continued toward Cherith, I saw
a shepherd standing among his sheep
at the door of the fold, anointing
their heads against the sun with oil,
the oil running from the horn like honey.
I remembered the Psalm of David
and my heart lifted up like a swallow.
East of the Jordan I saw a leper
by a stream, holding in one hand
two doves by their wing-tips and tails.
As I watched, he killed one bird
and caught its blood in a basin,
which he held over the running water.
So I stepped forward to bless him,
saying, 'Truly, you are clean.'
And I took the living bird from his hand
and dipped its breast into the basin,
dabbed its breast in the blood,
and let it go free. As it flew
I thought, There is hope for Israel yet;
for Israel, there is yet some hope.

The Raven

The raven is a black and craven bird,
a bird by the Law unclean.
Its carrion cry on the wind is heard—
the raven, that black and craven bird.
Yet it is the one the Lord by His word
has sent for my keep and keen.
Oh, the raven's a black and craven bird,
a bird by the Law unclean!

My Sweet Blackbirds

Aaah, we likes them. They has wings
like us, and feathers, too, them seraphim, them seraphs,
and they is white as our eyes is white.
Aaaw, caaaw, they is lovely, laaaverly, aaah!
And they is nice to us, yaaar, nice. Have some,
they says, have some. And they gives us meat,
lumpses of it. They doesn't toss it
likes we is yappy doggies or snorty piggy-pigs.
Naaa. They puts it right into our happy beakses,
puts it in, then pats us like what we likes.
Aaaw, nice. And they says, Have some more. Maaaw,
caaaw. Not so snappy, they says, but not snippy
or snaaarky, naaa. Kind of kind, they says it, kind of haaappy.
Not so snappy, they says, and they smiles
and squiggles us under the chinny-chin-chin,
like what we likes. Aaah, we says, naaa, nice.
Good ravens, they says, you can't helps it.
Can't, caaan't, we says. And they says,
Though you be foul, you be fowl without fault.
Haaa, funny fellaaas, them seraaaphs.
And they says, You was riven and driven from Eden
by fault of Adam, poor ravens. Yaaah, poor us,
we says. We's spotless, we's all shiny in our blackness.
Adam, he's the one. Aaadaaam, naughty,
naaasty, kaaa. And they gives us more juicy
lumpses, chunkses. Taaar, we says, taaar.
Not so snappy, they says. Manners, they says.
Never mind, they says, youse knows no better.
Aaah, we says, we knows lots. We knows
where the little sheepses is what say baaa, baaa.

And we knows their eyes is yummy
when they plops all bloody into the world
from their mummies. Aaaw, caaaw, maaaw!
No more of that, they says, them seraphs.
Look there, they says, and they points and bows
and we squiz up—and it's *Him*! Yahweh! Yaaahweh!
He is sunny-bright, but we sees him without squinting.
We sees Him. Our eyes fill up with Him
and our hearts go aaah in our throats, aaah.
And we hops onto His throne, and He lets us love Him
like He is our chick, our chickadee, our eggy
squawky daaarling. He chuckles like thunder,
very big booming, and he pats us and pets us.
Aaah, we says. Caaaw, laaaverly, aaah.
And he says, Go, my sweet blackbirds,
my black smoochies, go feed my prophet.
Then He says sort of twinkly, Fill your beaks
and follow my seraphs—they won't fly faaast
or faaar. Haaa, He's joking us! *Faaast or faaar!*
Haaa, we cackles, haaa! And we tips and flips
on our backses and waggles our leggses
and laughs and laaaughs our pecky beakses off.
And we caaaw *faaast* and we kaaa *faaar*
and we laaaugh, Haaa, good one, Yaaahweh!
And we is so happy we do some faaast flappings
and swift swooshings around His gleamy throne.
And He clapses and says, Oh, my sweet blackbirds,
my dark and stabby ravens, my daaarlings!

ix. Elijah

As with the Sky

I drank the water and tried not to think
of the people dying of thirst. At first
I thought the Lord had sent me to the brook
to save me. To save me from the king.
To save me from the drought. And surely
He had. But there was more. Three months
passed before I understood: He hid me
for their harm. My removal was
His retribution. The people were left
without a prophet. Yahweh abandoned them
to Baal. Leaving none to challenge
their choice, He confirmed them in it.
He gave them—oh, the horror!—He gave
them—oh, have mercy!—he gave them
the desires of their hearts! Truly He is
a holy God, and hard. He withdrew His word.
As with the sky, He shut up His mouth.
Body and soul, no bread for this people.

x. Elijah

By My Word

When Yahweh judges a nation,
even the righteous are reviled.
I do not know when it began but
one day I noticed—above my camp
where the water hung like a banner
over the balcony of stone—
a diminution. And downstream,
on a flat rock in the brook's bed,
on either side of the trickling
current, I saw a black crust on a stone
where once there had been slime
beneath a film of flowing water.
Then I realised, as if it were
a great revelation, that the brook
was drying. The source of my life
was failing for the drought
I had summoned by God's word
and could dismiss by mine. I watched
closely now and each day I saw
the stream narrow and the black,
crusty border widen. The frogs
stopped croaking. The small fish
no longer faced into the current
but circled aimlessly, penned
in small pools. I remembered the rock
Moses struck for water in the wilderness
and begged, 'Which rock, Lord,
shall I strike?' The white heron
shook its priestly plumage and
flew away. Finally, the ravens failed

to return. And still no word,
no whisper. But there was not silence.
I heard a voice that said, 'No rain
except by my word'. *MY word!*
I heard it again and again, until
I knelt and prayed for strength
not to pray for rain.

A Way of Escape

They set an ambush at the altar. Not all
Yahweh's prophets were present. We were less
than two hundred. We approached in procession,
the animals at the head. We set things in order.
Discipline and duty, ritual and righteousness,
symmetry and sanctity are betrothed at the altar
of the Lord. We began our worship. We cut
the calf's throat. I held the basin to catch
the blood. It gushed from the wound, thick
and steaming. I thought of sin and atonement.
I thought of the death I deserved, and pitied
the poor, guiltless heifer. As I stood to sprinkle
the sides of the altar, the prophets of Baal
stepped out of hiding—they rose up and ringed us
like bandits. They were Jezebel's prophets,
the whole four hundred from Samaria. We stared
in disbelief as they drew their daggers.
We were unarmed, save for the ceremonial knife.
I clung to the basin, swirling it out of habit
to keep the blood from congealing.
Someone bumped me and the crimson liquid
lapped over the rim onto my robe. It soaked
through the linen to my skin. It was very warm.

Then one the bandits stepped from the circle
into the centre and began to disrobe.
Our mouths were stopped. It was a woman.
It was the queen. It was Jezebel.
She wore jewellery and paint, like a prostitute—
only, never one so regal. Beneath the gauze

of her garments, she wore her body,
every curve and contour, with sensuous power
and assurance. Her flesh itself is a queen,
commanding fealty from men's hearts.
Even in our fear we felt the urge
to obey. Our eyes were at attention.

She said, Jezebel, our queen, 'There is a way
of escape. It is Elijah.' But we could not
betray the prophet. And I like to think
we *would not* have betrayed him,
even had we known where he was. Oh, Elijah!
Standing before her prophets, Jezebel
shone with savagery and sex. We lost
all hope and began to pray. In the onslaught
they passed me by. I stood, bewildered,
with the bowl in my arms, swirling the blood,
waiting to die. But when finally a bandit-prophet
attacked, I tossed the blood in his face.
It whooshed out, thin and sticky,
like heated honey. It struck his eyes.
I saw his eyelids peel back with the impact.
He dropped his dagger. I dropped the bowl and fled.

Thinking back, the scene has become
strangely symbolic. The sacrificial blood
did for my body what it should have done
for my soul. As physical proof of spiritual power,
it spread a covering, opened a way of escape.

The Meaning of My Name

When I first came
I knew it was not
enough. This brook
could not last
without rain. So why
was I shocked when
it failed? One year
I had waited in hiding,
one year in prayer,
one year studying
the Scroll and still
I was shaken.
The water failed.
The ravens fled.
Three days I was thirsty
until I remembered
the meaning of my name:
Elijah—Yahweh
is my strength.
You have taken the brook,
you have banished
the birds, yet will I wait
on your holy name.
And then His voice came:
'Go to Zarephath.'

xiii. Elijah

Two Things Unclean

'A widow in Zarephath will feed you.'
But I protested, 'Lord, it is a town
of Sidon of the Phoenicians. It is beyond
the borders of Israel, among the gentiles.
Are there not many widows in Israel, Lord?
Is none worthy to succour your servant?
First the ravens, now the pagans.
Lord, is there nothing holy for my help?

Behind the Glimpses

Since my husband died, I have been seeking
a saviour. Someone unlike Baal, who,
if his priests are true, is bloody and brutal.
And someone unlike Asherah, the goddess
of the groin, whom men worship with groans.
Men! They deify their desires! No, not
these gods. I have been seeking One who is
like … like nothing I have grasped but
many things I have glimpsed. As a girl,
I had a lamb that came when I called
its name. And I used to put flowers
in my hair—gathering them from the fields
that now, it seems, will never again be green.
Also, I remember how the rainbows
used to hurt my heart with their hints
of promises and purity. But not just
as a girl, though certainly it was keener,
cleaner, then. As a woman: our son
in my womb and later at my breast.
And the way my husband stroked my face
and smiled just before he died.
Yes, for all the grief, I've had glimpses.
This is the One I long for—the God
behind the glimpses. Someone good.
Someone who would make sense of life,
of living. Someone … Oh!
You know my meaning, or don't know, so
there's either no need or no way of telling.
One night I went to sleep, weeping,
and woke to the sound of a voice—

a soft, far voice like the stutter of a flame,
quiet, intermittent, quick—
that said, 'Soon. Soon.' I woke my son
and said, 'Soon, a deliverer.' But
it was a deception. In the morning,
it was hot. It has not rained
since. For a year, no rain. Our food
has dwindled. Soon, a slow death.
In the half-light of dawn this morning,
as I squatted by the ashes of the cooking fire,
a fly bothered me. When I waved it away,
the air unsettled the white ash,
which wafted and wobbled like goose-down
in the hearth. And as it shifted
I saw, briefly, for an instant only,
a small coal, bright as a rubbed ruby.
I claim no meanings. I simply say,
This morning I caught a glimpse of crimson,
a glimmer of warmth beneath the cold ashes.

Going to Zarephath

I followed the brook-bed down
to the Jordan River, drinking on the way
from puddles of brackish water.
The river was sluggish and turning
to salt. I washed as I crossed.
On the plain, with each step,
the dust spurted from my sandals
like spore from a puff-ball fungus.
It was hot. The air shifted
and shimmered above the parched land.
A raven perched on a carcass,
glistened blue-black as sin
on the rib-cage of a bull,
tugging a scrap of hide from a bone.
It cocked its head and winked
as I passed. At the outskirts
of the first town I approached,
two children fled from me, screaming.
Their strength failed well short
of the first house and they flopped
down exhausted. They lay panting
like small birds that have flown
too far in the heat. I strode
to them, stood over them, my shadow
shielding them from the scorching sun.
Their eyes were big in their gaunt faces.
Stick limbs and bloated bellies.
I tried to speak but no words came.
I stooped to caress their cheeks
but they croaked in horror.

I left them huddled on the hard
hot earth and skirted around the town.
Barely one year and already
the children and the animals ...
I journeyed on to the gentiles,
avoiding my own people on the way,
lest they should break my heart
and with it my resolve.

Gathering Sticks

I was gathering sticks by the city gate
when he came from the desert.
He looked dishevelled, dirty. He drew near
as if he knew me. Mad, I thought
and stepped back. Then he asked for water.
Water, of all things! But his voice defied
my definition. There was kindness there,
and courtesy. His accent announced
him as a Jew. There is a treaty
between our countries since our princess
slipped beneath a quilt to become
their queen. A compact but not compassion.
We have a history of hatred. Jeering
at Jews, some say, is one of life's joys.
And yet this man spoke with respect—
respect for me and for himself.
He neither begged nor bullied. He asked
for a drink in a way that made me
think I ought to thank him. The well
is within the walls. Quite a walk.
And yet I dropped my wood and went
willingly. Foreigners are forbidden water.
Unless, of course, they pay. Since
the drought, only citizens may draw it
free, though not freely. The rations
are stingy, the soldiers strict. But
I had yet to drop my bucket to fill my jar
for the day. It cost me nothing to save him
the money he did not have. I wanted
to do it. I felt a bond. We who are about

to die can at least be decent to each other.
Decency—it's one of the glimpses.
And so I dropped my sticks and turned back
to the gate. In the space of two steps
I remembered the voice—or did I hear it?—
'Soon. Soon.' And as my heart leapt
like a hart with thoughts of deliverance,
the man called out, 'And please,
make me also a cake to eat.' I staggered
with despair. My 'deliverer'? He brought nothing
but an empty belly for the last of my bread!

At the Sight of Her

She was gathering sticks by the city gate
when I arrived. My heart sank at the sight
of her. In doubt, I asked for a drink,
seeking the same sign of kindness
Eliezer sought from Rebecca. Yes,
she was the one. But it seemed wrong.
The widow was herself in want.
How could she help me? Had I heard amiss
God's voice? Nothing made sense.
'To Zarephath, which belongs to Sidon'.
Four days across the desert to a town
under the jurisdiction of Jezebel's
father. To a woman, and a widow
at that. And then to find her gathering
sticks to cook the last of her food.
It was against all reason. Yet what
is poverty except an opportunity
for the providence of God? Is His strength
limited by our weakness? Is His hand short
that it cannot save? He fed a nation
by the miracle of manna. Are three people
too many for Him? When I asked
the widow for food, she said, 'I have enough
for one meal for two—my son and me.'
Given the circumstance, there could be
no ignoring God's grace. By faith
I uttered an oracle. 'Fear not. The flour
and oil shall not fail, until the day
the Lord sends rain upon the earth.' Until,
by my word, the day of drenching.

Might not God multiply the oil without
the olive berry? Must He work only
through sap and seasons? May not He
bypass the tree? And the meal—must it
always come first from the ear and the mill?
'Fear not,' I said. Did she believe?
Perhaps. Or mayhap she thought it no longer
mattered. Whatever, she did as I bade—
brought water, baked a cake and gave it
to me. Steam rose like incense from its crust.
It tasted fine. It tasted like
the bread the ravens brought, only hot, hot.

One Meal More

I was wrong. There was enough
for three. I mixed the oil with the meal
and baked the dough on the coals.
I broke a piece for the prophet,
the remainder for my son and myself.
We ate in silence. He dabbed the crumbs
from his plate then asked for a place
to sleep. I prepared him a bed
in the room on the roof of the house.
When he'd settled I looked in the jar.
No oil, bar a film on the fired clay.
The barrel, too, was empty—merely
a dusting of flour on the floor. So, a liar
was lying in my bed, having eaten the last
of my bread. Shame on the shaman!
Shame on the fool who fell for his sham!
The oil spent, the flour failed, despite
every word he'd said. And yet at dusk
when he woke he asked for more.
More bread for his blasphemous mouth!
I lifted the lid to the jar. 'You said—'
I scoffed, then stopped. In the pot
was a cup of oil, glistening like honey
in the gloaming. And the flour—
three scoops in a heap in the barrel!
Though it ought to have been relief,
bitterness replaced my disbelief. True,
it was a miracle, but a mingy one
at best. In the face of months of famine,
the prophet's God, the mighty God
of Israel, gave from His bountiful store
barely enough for one meal more!

One Day at a Time

I used to sneak up and peep
into his room. Mostly he reads
or prays but sometimes he cries
like my mother sometimes cries,
without sound but with tears
running down. And sometimes
he groans like once I heard
a man groan when a soldier
stuck a sword into his stomach.
It frightens me still, his crying,
his groaning. One day when
I peeped in to find him praying,
he said, 'Yahweh, bless
the young scamp who is spying.'
I dashed downstairs but he didn't
scold or chase me, so I came back.
He looked up and beckoned.
I went in and sat on his bed-roll
and he read to me from the scroll.
He reads to me a lot. The bit
I like best is about the manna,
the bread that fell from heaven
at night to feed the Israelites.
They could only keep enough
for one day. It stank if they tried
to store it. 'Why couldn't they
keep it?' I asked him once.
He said, 'One day at a time—
that's enough to feed the body
and keep the spirit hungry.'

Ahab's Envoy

There had been rumours for some time
that Ahab was sending envoys to the nations
to seek me out. And to Ethbaal also
he sent a messenger. This day,
a rider came to Zarephath, on his way
from Tyre to Sidon, having followed
the coast road. His mount's
mane was braided with silver bells;
a truce banner flew from his pommel;
and he wore the royal insignia of Israel
on his quiver and breastplate. He arrived
at the gate as the widow was going out
for wood. She heard him speak
to the soldiers. A Hebrew accent,
like mine. She ran home empty-handed,
distressed. I was not alarmed:
whom the Lord hides, no man can reveal;
and whom He reveals, no man can hide.
Then we heard the horse's hooves
on the pavement of our street. I peered
through the window and the same instant
the mount rolled its eyes and reared up.
The rider fell headlong. The gelding,
still standing on its hind legs, stepped back
onto the man's neck. I heard it crack.
The governor of the town was distraught.
And what to do? Send the corpse
to Ethbaal at Sidon or to Ahab at Samaria?
To avoid suspicion, both kings
needed to see the body. Yet decay,

its disfigurement and stench, seemed
bound to offend one king or the other.
It was hot. The wind was a bellows
to fan the sun's furnace. What to do?
Taking advice, the governor laid the body
in a box, which he filled with honey.
And so the messenger began his last journey
lying in amber liquid, embalmed by bees.
Never was a man's death so sweet.

xxi. Elijah

Death

I was in my room, dozing,
when I heard her scream.
The widow, her death-wail.
It was all so sudden, un-
expected. I rose quickly
and staggered for the door,
feeling dizzy from the abrupt
movement. I held the wall
to steady myself as I stumbled
down the steps. I've heard it
often since coming to Zarephath—
the sound of death
as it tears a mother's heart
out through her throat.
God knows, I've heard it
often, but mostly from afar—
a house or a street away—
as the famine feasts
on another bloated belly.
But now the death-cry came
from my own lodging house,
the house of sanctuary.
I opened the door and
stepped into the darkness.
The boy was dead,
dead in his mother's arms.
She stopped her wailing
and stared at me. I waited.
Then she spoke, accusing me,
cursing me. Dear Lord,

does my presence herald
your judgment as a trumpet
heralds a king? I wanted
to kneel, to plead for pardon.
Instead, I stepped to her
and said, 'Let me have him.'
She neither gave him
nor resisted when I took him.
I carried him out to the sunlight,
up the stairs and into
the shadows of my empty room.

Accusation

In my grief, I said dreadful things
to the prophet. Dreadful! It seemed
all the faith I had learnt from him
had turned to fear and grief and hate.
I thought: This is his doing. The prophet
has killed my son in payment
for my sins. I thought of my neighbours
and of the women of Israel whose sons
were dead because this man of God
had staunched the rain and stopped the grain.
And all this because they had worshipped
Baal, the god I too once served.
I am no better than my sisters,
I thought, and this prophet and his God
have known it all along. They have
fattened me with friendship
as a herdsman fattens his swine
for the slaughter. And so
I said dreadful things to him. Dreadful!
He listened, looking always at my boy,
then said when I was silent, 'Give him
to me.' He took him from my bosom,
carried him up into his room
and closed the door, kicked it shut,
leaving me with only the memory
of my son's arm drooping to the floor,
the hand graceful as a *qedishim* dancer.
I went in and he ordered me out.
But as I sat on the steps, waiting,
a calm came upon me, a confidence

in the prophet. And I remembered
what he had said about the Day of Atonement,
the blood of the lamb blotting out
the sins of those who repent.
Surely the prophet's God knows no guile.
Surely He forgets the sins He forgives.
The Almighty, the Allknowing remembers
them no more. He alone has the power
for it, for the forgetting.

Resurrection

He was heavy, a deadweight.
I was panting by time I reached
my room. I had enough breath
for two. I lay him on my bed,
arranged his head, his limbs
in a semblance of order—
doing those little things
the dead can no longer do
for themselves—straightening
a kink in his wrist,
resettling his head on the pillow,
out of the backward bend
that would have hurt his neck
were he alive. Already
he was beginning to stiffen.
I cried to the Lord, the God
of mercies. I lay upon the boy,
head to head, hand to hand,
chest to chest. His mother
blundered into the room. I had
no time to reason. I ordered,
'Get out! Close the door!'
She went and I rose and knelt
in prayer. A second time
I stretched upon him.
I had in mind the number three—
the number of God, the number
of perfection and power.
The third time I did not rise
from the corpse but pressed

myself to him as I prayed:
'Lord, send his soul again.'
Then his chest rose like a boat
on a swell and his arms
reached round my neck to hug me.

Redemption

He did not speak on the first day.
On the second, he climbed to my room
and stood at my door. I beckoned
with a nod and he stepped in,
stood back a pace, and spoke:
'Father, I saw the face of the angels
who stand before the Light of God.'
So, he had seen in person
what I had seen only in visions.
I felt, I am ashamed to say, envious.
I said, 'And what did you do?
What did you feel?' He turned pale
and trembled. 'I felt afraid.
I fell on my face and felt
the dread of a second death.' Oh,
had I erred to retrieve him? Had I
stripped him of the raiment of eternity
and clothed him again in the rags
of mortality. 'You have come back,'
I said, touching his hair, his face,
to comfort him. 'You had a premonition
of living to die again. You feared
what I have done.' He shook his head.
'No, father. It was more. Always dying.
You saved me from Always Death.'
Then I understood his meaning
and God's mercy, understood
he had gone into judgment
and yet was spared justice.
This boy will have two chances at Life
for the price of two passing deaths.

Circumcision

For five more days we spoke, the boy and I,
about the things of God. On the eighth day,
the day of the completion of his conversion,
I took him aside, apart from his mother,
as in Israelite will take his infant son
eight days from birth, and circumcised him,
cutting the foreskin according to the Covenant,
making in his penis the mark of purity
and promise. He is too young yet
to know the power of seed surging
in the loins. But he will learn
soon enough. Where the desire is strongest,
so too are the distortions of sin and
the demands of holiness. After I'd cut him
and cleaned up the blood, I taught him:
'I have done in your flesh what God
has done in your heart. You are now
a citizen of Israel, an heir to Heaven.
In the depths and heights of life,
this is a reminder of your Redeemer.
To the honour of the Lord of Hosts, you are
sealed by a scar at the source of life,
healed by a wound in the place of passion.'

At the Heart of His Heart

I am overseer of the King's palace and know
his majesty's mind in all matters. The Queen
is at the heart of his heart and that
is why he is heartless. The hand of the Lord
is heavy upon him, yet he will not repent.
His heart hardens in the heat of the drought
like a brick in a kiln. The people starve,
yet he staves off compassion. He frets
for fodder for his horses. Having spurned
his Sovereign, he slights his subjects.
When King David sinned and the nation suffered,
he pleaded with the Lord for the people, saying,
'Lo, I have sinned, I have done wickedly,
but these sheep, what have they done?
Let your hand, I beg you, be against me alone.'
Truly, David was a man after God's own heart.
But Ahab, my master, whom I serve before the Lord
in all honour, is a man after Jezebel's heart.

Waiting

At Cherith and at Zarephath it was not
three and a half years that I waited.
It was one thousand two hundred and
seventy seven days. And each day
I tried to remember that waiting
is a great work when it is in
the Lord's will. Though an axle
is fixed, it permits the wheel to spin
and is carried along in turn.
Though it seem so, the Lord is not slow
to fulfil His purposes: He knows
no haste to achieve His plans. And yet
it was hard to keep still, to stay
at the centre of His will—hard
not to think that to wait
is to waste time and opportunity.
Daily I prayed as Moses prayed: Lord,
so teach me to number my days,
that I may apply my heart to wisdom.
And it came to pass after many days
the word of the Lord came to me: 'Go,
show yourself to Ahab.'
And I was glad to be going: action
at last! But I was sad, too,
to be leaving the widow and the boy.
I knew I would never see them again.
And there was in my heart also
a touch of fear: 'Show yourself,'
He said. It was like a taunt,
a taunt to the king who craved to kill me.

Sanctuary

We used to debate about him—Obadiah, the lord high
chamberlain of the palace. Many said he was a good man.
'Not so good as to leave the court,' I said.
How quick we are to condemn! How easily we judge
matters too high and too deep for us! It repents me.
Once, another prophet warned me: 'Beware. Who knows
whether he has not come to the kingdom for such a time
as this?' I scoffed. I remember it with shame.
I said with that peculiar venom of the self-righteous,
'Who can please the king of Israel and the King of Heaven
both? God is of purer eyes than to look upon evil.
How, then, can He behold a man in Ahab's palace?'
It repents me. I am turned over, like a cart
on a mountain pass. And then the prophets of Baal
slaughtered the prophets of Yahweh at Shilo. I alone
escaped. And as I fled towards Bethel,
a chariot overtook me. I thought it was death
but it was Obadiah. He caught me up and carried me
to sanctuary—this cave, with its great caverns
and echoes and blackness. We are one hundred now—
five-score prophets, the remnant, cloistered in a cave
by the kindness of Obadiah. He delivered us,
not by the goodness of his character alone, but
by the greatness of his power as the king's captain.
True to his name—'Servant of Yahweh'—he serves
where the Sovereign Lord has set him. Oh, Obadiah,
forgive my obduracy! You have crushed the asp
of my arrogance. You have milked the venom from my mouth.

The King's Horses

The king has two thousand chariots:
four hundred he keeps in Samaria
and the rest in the chariot cities
of Hazor, Megiddo and Gezer. His stables
stand four thousand horses. His herds
hold more horses still. No war
has troubled the kingdom since Elijah
confronted the king. This is God's
only grace. In the first year
of famine, Ahab rode his chariot
for sport, hunting lions and gazelle.
He was wounded that year by a lioness,
which, enraged by an arrow in its throat,
leapt onto the backs of his stallions
and sprang at him, claws unsheathed.
His chariot lord saved him, jabbing
the beast through with a javelin.
The cat's blood mingled with the king's
on the floor of the chariot. An omen,
some said. Game became scarce as straw.
He stopped hunting in the second year.
In the third, the horses began to starve
—except for those in the king's stall.
Their coats lost their sheen, became angular
like rugs spread on rocky ground.
And Ahab said to me, 'Go through the land
to all the springs and valleys.
Perhaps we may find grass to save
the horses.' I went as bidden, driving
a chariot towards the Valley of Jezreel.

Megiddo

On my way from Zarephath to Samaria,
I stopped at Megiddo, the fortified city
Joshua captured from the Canaanites
and Solomon strengthened for his chariots
and Ahab enlarged for his stores. Megiddo,
that commands the pass to the Valley
of Jezreel. I was not challenged
as I entered the gates. In truth,
though I walked right by them, the guards
did not seem to see me. The city
was dilapidated, the citizens dispirited.
The storehouses were empty:
not a pot of oil, not a skin of wine.
Only two store-rooms were guarded,
their doors shut and barred.
In the stables the horses were dejected,
heads hanging, bones protruding
through their hides. And the chariots
were in disrepair. I followed a woman
down the steps of a deep shaft
and along a tunnel beneath the city wall
to a cave where a spring was gushing.
I drank after the woman had filled her jar.
In the sunlight again, I squinted
into the storage-pit in front
of the south palace. It was empty,
a hole in the ground walled with stone,
like an enormous well-shaft.
The pit the king boasted could hold
13,000 sacks of grain, empty, not even

a scattering of seed on the floor,
only the random droppings of pigeons,
like little cakes baked by the sun.
Someone bumped me as I looked in
and I almost fell. I clutched at the air
to save myself. I stepped back, filled
with a sudden fear of a futile death.
If I must die, let it be at Ahab's hand.

Mandrake

Midway between Megiddo and Samaria
I saw a woman carrying a mandrake,
the yellow fruit dangling in a cluster
from her slender hand. Embarrassed,
she averted her eyes as I approached.
I said, 'Shalom.' She glanced
at me and then at the love apples.
'For my husband,' she said, blushing.
I nodded. We were standing now,
face to face, the dust of our walking
settling at our feet. She needed
to speak. 'You are a holy man,'
she said, gazing at me directly.
'Can you help?' I shook my head.
'I am not a healer.' Her shoulders
slumped and she looked away.
She was young and the little
I could see of her face above the veil
was pleasing, but her skirts
were loose as a Bedouin tent,
so I could not tell. I asked,
'Are you beautiful?' She said,
'I don't know, lord.' 'What does
your husband say?' 'He says, Yes.'
Then her eyes filmed and she shook
her head. 'He used to say so
but now he goes to the temple,
to the *qedishim*.' Because of Baal
men turn from beauty to perversity.
I would need no aphrodisiac

had I such a wife. I wanted
to wipe the tears from her cheeks.
And I suddenly yearned
to be like other men, to know
the softness and comfort of a wife.
Oh, Lord, your way is so lonely!
I said to the woman, 'Tonight,
when you go in to him, after
he has drunk the potion and looked
upon you, while the lamp is still
burning, read him the Song of Songs.
It is passionate and pure. Perhaps
it will help.' She said, 'What is it?'
My voice, I think, did not betray
my astonishment. 'The Song
of Solomon to the Shulammite.
From the Scriptures.' It meant
nothing to her. She was puzzled.
I said, 'Do you have a priest?'
She said, 'Of Baal or Asherah?'
'No. Of Yahweh.' She shook her head.
'Then,' I said, 'there is no help.'

xxxii. Obadiah

When I Found the Prophet

I was in my chariot, searching for pasture,
when I found the prophet. I was halfway
to Megiddo, driving slowly to conserve
the horses, when I saw him on the road.
A woman was walking away from him.
The distance between us contracted slowly,
like a strip of raw leather drying
in the sun. When I recognised him,
I flicked the reins. The horses flinched
but would not canter. I leapt out, ran
and fell at his feet. 'Is it you, my lord?'
He lifted me with his right hand and said,
'Go tell your lord, "Behold, Elijah is here."'
Would that he had left me down in the dust.
He lifted me only to slay me! For three years
the potentate has pursued the prophet.
Now he comes with a casual command. Truly,
terror awaits those who taunt a tyrant.
And he would make *me* the instrument
of his insult! Oh have mercy, holy man!
Even on foot he would be far in the hills
before I returned. Then whose blood,
whose blood would slake the king's fury?
I have seen him murder his messengers
for failing to find the prophet. Last week
he tore the tongue from the envoy from Egypt
who brought bad news of no news of Elijah.
And now at a whim he deigns to appear
to command me to tell Ahab, 'Elijah is here.'

Read more of Andrew Lansdown's poetry in...

Birds in Mind
Australian Nature Poems

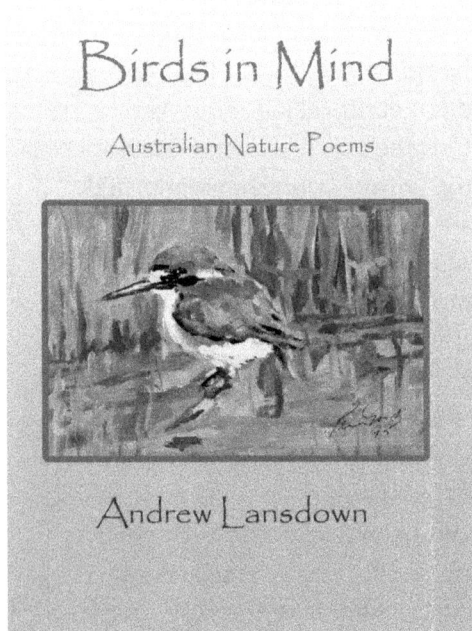

Order direct from the publisher, Wombat Books, or
through your local bookstore.

www.wombatbooks.com.au/birdsinmind.html

www.ingramcontent.com/pod-product-compliance
Lightning Source LLC
Chambersburg PA
CBHW071423090426
42737CB00011B/1550